The Greatest Part of Me

~*~*~*~*~*~*~*~*~*~*~

Evangelist Shanetria Y. Peterson

SENSATIONAL CHRISTIAN CREATIONS PUBLISHING
Rapides Island, Louisiana 71409

Unless otherwise indicated, Scripture quotations in this book is taken from the Holy Bible, KJV Version All Rights Reserved.Copyright 1979 by Holman Bible Publishing. Nashville, TN 37234.

This is a true story, and names have not been used to identify certain individuals to protect their identity and privacy.

Cover Design by: Shanetria Peterson

The Greatest Part of Me and Now It's Time for Deliverance
Copyright 2006 by Sensational Christian Creations
Rapides Island, Louisiana 71409

ISBN: 978-0-6151-6130-3

All rights reserved. No portion of this book may be reproduced in any form without the written permission of the publisher.

Printed in the United States of America

Dedication:

I dedicate this book to my family and all those women and men in the

body of Christ

that have been through a storm, but have had the diligence to come out

of their

storm through Jesus Christ.

To all who may have the opportunity to read this book, I pray that it blesses you tremendously. Through all of my trials, tribulations, and setbacks, I have found the greatest part of me. I pray that you are blessed deep down in your spirit as I tell part of my personal testimony along with the joy of finding Jesus Christ in the midst of my trials and tribulations. This book is dedicated to me, for through the years, I have been silent about many things, but no longer will I be silent about my past.

I thank God for being my anchor as I continue to walk in my deliverance from sexual bondages, I have decided that I will not be silent any longer. My daughter is a great blessing to me and although she was conceived out of wedlock, I don't regret for one second, having her in my life. She makes me smile when I don't feel like smiling, and without her in my life, I don't know what I would do because she is my sunshine and I'm glad to be her mother. Most importantly of all, without Jesus in my life, I would not be here to tell you my story. So brace yourself for the long haul, you're in for a ride.

The Lord is my Shepherd, I shall not want. He maketh me to lie down in green pastures. He leadeth me beside the still waters. He restoreth my soul. He leadeth me in the path of righteousness for his name sake. Ye, thou I walk through the valley of the shadow of death, I will fear no evil, for thou are with me. Thy rod and thy staff shalt comfort me. Thou preparest a table before me in the presence of my enemy. Thou anoinest my head with oil, my cup runneth over. Surely goodness and mercy shall follow me all the days of my life, and I shall dwell in the house of the Lord forever Psalms 23 KJV.

I am learning how to walk worthy according to God's perfect will in my life. I knew yall early on that I had a purpose even as a child. I got ran over by a car at the age of four years and escaped with my life and just a bruise on my right arm that to this day, bares the mark of that horrible and eventful day. I was underneath the tires of that car that ran over me, do yall hear me? My parents thought I was gone, but was amazed when I jumped from under the car unharmed (except for the bruise), completely in tears. I know now that it was purpose...purpose...purpose. "Ye, thou I walk through the valley of the shadow of death, I fear no evil for thou art with me." God pulled me through that ordeal, and although I was four at the time, I still remember that day as though it happened yesterday and the relief that came over my family when they realized I was okay. I have been through many ordeals in my life, from battling an eating disorder at age 15, (bulimia), and hid it for many years from my family. I also sufferered severe depression spells where I would withdraw from everyone and would cry for hours at a time with no apparent motive.

Women, I don't care how good of an experience you think a man can give you, there's nobody on this earth that can give you the love and the pleasure that you're seeking like Jesus can! Learn to walk worthy according to his will! Surely goodness and mercy shall follow me all the days of my life and I shall dwell in the house of the Lord forever! As time wore on, I was in and out of relationships with ex boyfriends and boyfriends I was hooking up with...I'm not going to go into every little detail of my life story here, but I pray just this little bit helps somebody. I have heard the words; I love you so many times. I have heard the words, I will never leave you so many times that I can't count on my fingers, but women I LEARNED, that Jesus is the only man that will never leave you nor forsake you. I have gone back to my first love and my life is lining up according to his purpose for me! His love will never ever wax cold! I don't care what you have battled with in your life-time; God has a divine purpose for you! You may be living with HIV/ AIDS, an STD that you have to deal with for life, but you can live with those diseases today if you learn your PURPOSE. The LORD will lead you in the path of righteousness for his name sake! Walk in his perfect will for your life, for you are a testimony to the world and to the Devil that you are indeed a survivor. I don't care what that serpent is whispering in your ear right now, you are redeemed and set free from his grips! Learn to walk worthy in your callings and hold your head up high, for the Lord thy God, IS your Shepherd and YOU shall not WANT!

I really don't know where to begin, but I can begin with the most important part of this testimony and that's finding Jesus Christ through all of my struggles with sexual sins. The devil want many of us to be silent on the bondages that we used to be in. By being "silent," that's his way of holding our past over our heads, but it's time for us to come out of our silence and help someone else who may be traveling down a similar pathway to destruction. As a child I came from a close knit family. I always felt isolated and alone although I knew that I wasn't. My parents made sure they brought us up in the fear of the Lord although at the time, I didn't think that it was Godly fear. I realize now that my parents had flaws just like any other parents, and most things they thought they were doing to protect us. As a teenager, I began to experience peer pressure and had the desires to do many things that my so-called friends were doing. I knew not to get tangled up in alot of things growing up. I don't want to talk about all of the details in my book, but just summarize some parts of my story.

I met my baby's Father who was different from the rest of the guys that I had ever dated. He was older so I perceived there was authentic interest there. That relationship was like none other. I had actually met someone that treated me nice. He took me out to eat, he brought me things, he took me places, but I learned he was in a relationship with a woman of 7 years. He was telling me that things were not going well with her, and like a fool, I believed his lies....

I kept going on in this bondage with this man in hopes that he would leave this woman of 7 years to be with me...After awhile, I got tired of giving my body to a man that obviously was not going anywhere. So I gave him a choice to either leave this woman or lose me. You may as well guess. "He didn't leave this woman..." I broke off the relationship with him, and began to go on with my life. I was starting to get my relationship with God back on track. I had a long way to go, but I was determined to get my life back right. Notice here I didn't say that I allowed God to get my life back on track. I tried to do it in my own strength and it eventually crumbled through. That was a big mistake there because God is the only one that can clean us up. He didn't give us the willpower to do it on our own. After about three weeks of not having any contact with my baby's father, he up and called me out of the blue and told me that the woman was gone. I didn't believe him, until he said he was going to prove it to me. So after that, he began to pick me up and I started spending time at his home. I realized that she was indeed gone. Her clothes were still in the house, but he said he was going to put them out in the garage closet so she could come and get them. I moved in with him and we began to have a steady relationship. My parents were truly shocked that I was doing this, but I felt that I loved this man. The world does confuse lust with love...and now as I look back over this, I realize that it was lust that I was in! Well, this man started staying out all times of night, and not even calling to say where he was. He had an eight year old handicapped son that he would leave me home with while he did his dirty work. I suspected that I was pregnant, but didn't get a test done.

I started immediately taking precautions just in case I was. I had stopped drinking and smoking cigarettes, but some days out of frustration and anger at my baby's father, I would occasionally drink. I was obviously trying to do the right thing. I was being faithful, and although I had men that wanted to get with me while I was with him, I didn't slip up. I was serious about making this relationship work. We talked about marriage, and that was a big jump because usually, he wouldn't discuss anywhere near that subject. So, as the days flew by, I started preparing to become this man's wife. One day, things changed....I had enrolled in college for Business to get my degree. I resigned from my old job to attend school full-time. The plan "was that I was going to be riding with my mother and staying at their house during the week-day and return home on the weekends since he did not want to get up in the mornings to bring me to my mom's house and then rush back to get his son ready for school." Needless to say, that may have been his plan to get rid of me. During that time, I suspected that he was cheating, but just didn't have the evidence to back up my claim.

Bear with me, because it is very hard to talk about this, but I'm determined....One day while at my mom's house...on a Saturday morning as a matter of fact, I was waiting for him to come and get me. It took him the longest to come that particular morning. I had clothes to wash and since we didn't have our own washer and dryer, I used moms to wash my clothes, and he would also take some to the washateria. Well, I waited with my pillow case of clean clothes for him to come pick me up. He was late as usual, but he came. I knew something was very fishy, but I didn't say anything. When we arrived home, I went to the bedroom and found the covers pulled back...Usually our bed was neatly kept...and never was the covers pulled all the way to the end unless we were having intercourse...seeing those covers pulled back, I just stopped and stared....but I still didn't say anything. We went to bed and as I lay my head down on my pillow, I smelled cheap perfume on my pillowcase. I immediately sat up and began to sniff. I only wear the best of perfumes and I am very articulate about my appearance, the way I dress and especially my scents! This was not my perfume on my pillowcase, so when I began to sniff, he also sat up and said..."What?"

I didn't say anything, but lay back down. He had told me earlier that he had to work...Saturday was his off-day and HE NEVER WORKS AN OFF DAY!

My suspicions grew, but I played right along with him. We drifted off to sleep, and before 2:00 rang around, we got up and I got dressed to go to my parent's house. He dropped me off and said that he was going to come back and get me.

I told him to make sure that he did because I didn't have any clothes there at my mom's. He told me that he would and that he would call me later. All through that day, I hadn't heard anything from him, so around about 7 or 8 o'clock, I decided to call him at work to find out how come he didn't call. Well, guess what? I was told what I had already knew "he didn't work that day!" So, I started calling the house but wouldn't receive an answer. Finally, I called and a woman answered the phone. I was like in my mind: "I must have dialed the wrong number," so I dialed the number again, and this time, he answered! I asked him who answered that phone the first time I had called. He told me that "Debra was over to the house..." Debra was supposedly his best friend that he was being a shoulder for because she was in an abusive relationship with her husband.

My suspicions rose higher. I told him to come and get me because I was ready to go and that I didn't have any clothes. He told me that he would come later...I then confronted him about not being at work, and he totally denied it. I kept begging him to come and get me so I can get my clothes, and finally he said, "I'm going to come get you in the morning." That did it!!!!! One thing I don't like is wearing clothes all day long and then sleeping in them! My brother's best friend was at the house. I stormed up to the front of the house out of my old room and told my brother's best friend to come and take me home. I knew the scenery that I was going to walk in on, but I wanted to catch him in his lie! On the drive to the house, I kept looking out of the window at the full moon. I just couldn't believe that I had let this man deceive me for so long. Before my brother's friend car pulled up to the house after giving directions, I pulled out my keys. I calmly got out of the car and walked to the door. The house was dark so I knew that they were gone to bed.

I unlocked the door and went in. I turned on the kitchen light. No one was in the front room, so I walked all the way to the bedroom to the back. His little boy was lying on the floor in his room, and when he saw me, he looked up and stared at me. In haste, I opened our bedroom door on the right and turned on the light and there were those two so called best friends: in the bed....

I can't go on with everything else that happened in that encounter, but just know I got all of my clothes and items that night and left...the items that I left that night, they remained. That was a very disheartening experience. I discovered I was nearly three months pregnant after that experience (what I had already suspected), I went though my pregnancy without him, and had a beautiful baby girl. My baby is almost four years old and he has only seen her once since she's been in this world...

He never calls her, he doesn't ask about her, but the only thing he does is send child support when he feels like it. Since that time in my life, I had tried to put my life on track. I entered into relationships that were adding hurt on top of hurt. I was engaged to be married to my best friend from college, but after a few months, he told me he wasn't ready for marriage. I had just lost my grandmother. I was very close to her, and then to have my engagement broken, I was bleeding on the inside. In the process of starting to heal, I met a man online....during this bondage, I got caught up in things that I never done before...I did think of the fact that Matthew 12:43-45 **KJV** says; When the unclean spirit is gone out of a man, he walketh through dry places, seeking rest, and findeth none. 44 Then he says,' I will return into my house from which I came out,' and when he has come back, he finds it empty, swept, and put in order.

45 Then he goes, and takes with himself seven other spirits more evil than he is, and they enter in and dwell there. The last state of that man becomes worse than the first. Even so will it be also to this evil generation."

I got caught up in things that I have never done before. (I will not go into all of the details for it's a shame to even speak of those things that are done in darkness). I had made a vow to God after having my baby that I was not going to have sex until I married. Although this wasn't the physical act, I was committing adultery in my heart with men that weren't my husband.... (That's just as dangerous as the physical act outside of marriage!) I was in sexual lust with this man I was full of it and it seemed every time that I talked with this man, those strong feelings of lust seemed to overpower me. Throughout our brief relationship, he was telling me that he was divorced, and so I trusted him without verifying the information that he was telling me about himself. He would call all times of the day, but he told me to never call his home because he didn't want his kids involved in this for (protection purposes) he claimed he wasn't ready to introduce them to another woman. I believed his lies...and as time went along, I found out that this man was a habitual liar and was a **narcissist**. (You can look that up in a dictionary and find out the character traits of a narcissist), I was depressed about being a single mother and barely making ends meet...I felt guilty for all of the past things that I had done, but yet, I felt like I couldn't get out of sexual bondage.....I started having nervous break-downs...all the while, the narcissist kept making me false promises that he couldn't keep...I was weighted down with hurt, guilt, and sin from my past pouring into this piece of a relationship that I had with this man.

This man was sending me money to help me and my daughter out, and I felt like a charity case. I didn't want to live like this any longer. My health was starting to suffer as well as my self-esteem....All the while, I felt the presence of God around me even though I was in sin, but one day, I got so tired and stressed...after ending the relationship with the narcissist, I entered another one with a professed Christian, after finding out that he was playing games, I was at my lowest. After the last nervous break down, I decided enough was enough! I sought my deliverance after all of this.

 I know there are some of you that may be ashamed to talk about your past, but if you are a Christian, getting those unshed feelings out helps you as well as others. I was called into the ministry at 7 months pregnant, but wasn't ready. It's like reading a horror story as I reread this page. It's a blessing to say that "I'm saved today," but not only am I'm saved, I'm delivered from my horrific past. I occasionally still struggle with the guilt and the emotions, but as time goes along, I'm healing. Over the years many of us accumulate sin and get enslaved in bondages of the devil adding sin on top of sin. When I learned about deliverance, I learned that there was more to our walks than just accepting Jesus as Lord and Savior and receiving salvation. Many Christians are saved, but not delivered from bondages of the devil. After the Holy Ghost ministered to me on the subject of deliverance, I wrote a book that I pray will help others realize their need for deliverance from bondages of all kinds. I thank God for allowing me to tell my story of healing and deliverance in this book.

My desire is that my testimony will help someone else to realize that no matter how big of a sinner you think you may be, Jesus can and will pick you up and set you free. I was scared that I wouldn't find a man that would not judge me by my past, but I thank God that I stopped looking. I really thank God for the book, "I kissed Dating Goodbye." Although I haven't read it, the title speaks for my life currently. This is not nearly all of my testimony, but I only covered and summarized the areas that I could. I pray that you are blessed by it. As you could see, I'm not ashamed to tell where God had brought me from. I haven't been saved all of my life. In order to help others, I feel I must tell them where I've been before telling them where I'm going. Although this testimony is quite graphic, it's placed here in this book to help someone else. I am proud to say that I am an overcomer and I do not desire to go through anything like I have gone through anymore. Doing things outside of God's originated plan hurts you in the long run. The past always has a way of coming back and haunting you, but at least your soul doesn't have to perish in a burning hell when you're saved and delivered. Although I'm saved, I have to walk around some days with occasional guilt and consequences; (in which I feel is a thorn in my flesh as a reminder). I thank God that I'm healing emotionally as each new day passes. Man think you can just wake up one morning and you're healed emotional without going through a process. God takes us through a cleansing and renewal process and he sets us apart unto holiness. (sanctification)... and he's the only one that can heal all bleeding wounds. I cannot get my virginity back, but one thing I can and will continue to take back, and that's territory that the devil has stolen from me. I arise with no more chains and shackles. I'm no longer a slave to sexual sins and bondages. God set me free to help others and I'm blessed to be here today to tell my story. I do not care about negative and bad things that people may say or think about me. I'm using my deliverance to help others who may be traveling down a similar path to encourage them that there is hope only in Jesus Christ. 1 Peter 4:12-13 reads; 12Beloved, think it not strange concerning the fiery trial which is to try you, as though some strange thing happened unto you:

13But rejoice, inasmuch as ye are partakers of Christ's sufferings; that, when his glory shall be revealed, ye may be glad also with exceeding joy. I do believe that it will be a rewarding experience if I continue to hold on and keep the faith in God and learn how to embrace humility. Those of you that have been in the wilderness for however long...it Doesn't matter....I want to encourage you to Lift up your heads, O ye gates; even lift them up, ye everlasting doors; and the King of glory shall come in. Psalm 24:9 God knows that you are weary, he has seen your tears, he knows all about your struggles, but lift up your voice and say: "He will not leave me like he found me." There's a praise in your belly just waiting to come forth....many of you are waiting until the battle is over to shout, but the time to be shouting is right now!!!!! Start declaring the victory over your life right now! Open your mouth and let the Holy Ghost have his way through you. It's time to stop looking at your situation in the natural....It's time to start focusing on the supernatural. You can't claim one thing and you still looking at your present circumstance in the natural with a hopeless, disgruntled attitude! It's time to put those attitudes in check; you got to learn to endure humility. Somebody about to go to the next level in God, will it be you?

1   Ps.55:17 (KJV)

Evening, and morning, and at noon, will I pray, and cry aloud: and he shall hear my voice.

2   Humble yourselves before the Lord, and he will lift you up. (James 4:10)

3   This is the one I esteem: He who is humble and contrite in spirit, and trembles at my word. (Isaiah 66:2)

4   For everyone who exalts himself will be humbled, and he who humbles himself will be exalted. (Luke 14:11)

He chose the lowly things of this world and the despised things - and the things that are not - to nullify the things that are, so that no one may boast before him. (I Corinthians 1:28-29)

1 So neither he who plants nor he who waters is anything, but only God, who makes things grow. (1 Corinthians 3:7)

2 Do nothing out of selfish ambition or vain conceit, but in humility consider others better than yourselves. (Philippians 2:3)

3 Honor one another above yourselves. (Romans 12:10)

4 All of you clothe yourselves with humility toward one another, because, "God opposes the proud, but gives grace to the humble." (1 Peter 5:5)

5 For we do not preach ourselves, but Jesus Christ as Lord, and ourselves as your servants for Jesus' sake. (2 Corinthians 4:5)

6 So you also, when you have done everything you were told to do, should say, "We are unworthy servants; we have only done our duty." (Luke 17:10)

7 Your attitude should be the same as that of Christ Jesus: Who, being in very nature God, did not consider equality with God something to be grasped, but made himself nothing, taking the very nature of a servant, being made in human likeness.

(Philippians 2:5-7)

8   Humility and fear of the LORD bring wealth and honor and life. (Proverbs 22:4)

9   You save the humble but bring low those whose eyes are haughty. (Psalm 18:27)

10 But the meek will inherit the land and enjoy great peace. (Psalm 37:11)

I know it's hard and the situation is rather uncomfortable...but in order to be humble, you must suffer some tough and uncomfortable situations! Saints, God must get the glory in your life...If he would have been quick in blessing you; some of you would have taken the glory for all that he has done....you had to go through a season of humility because some people want the blessings, but they want it the (quick and easy way)...they don't want to suffer, they don't want to take on the sufferings of Jesus Christ and know him in the likeness of his death, burial, and resurrection.

No cross no crown! This is a quickie generation. Everybody want things quick and easy, but no one wants to labor for it...they don't want to trust God for anything anymore. They do not want to go through humility and find God in it! This is a season of reclaiming what rightfully belongs to you, but if you don't want to humble yourself in order to receive it...and if you don't want to come out of the works of the flesh in order to walk this walk in victory, then you will stay stagnant and will forever be the enemy's prey...... (Hmmmmm....that's not fun now is it?)

There's more to this life than materialistic blessings...for those things will fade away, but why not get something down in your spirit that's going to sustain and keep you even after you die and leave this earth!!!! Let me elaborate, if you live your life honoring God in body, mind, and spirit....If you live your life being obedient to God, loving what he loves and hating what he hates....you will get total victory just like Christ did....but see you know what most of the church's problem is? Some people still want to hang on to the ways of the world and still try to walk in the victory of Jesus Christ. What's wrong with that picture? Holiness and filth don't have one thing in common....This is not burger king have it your way.....You must be one way or no way at all...There are no in-between's...

There are preachers telling their flock to name it and claim it, but some of these people are living shabby and filthy!!!! Now how can God show up in garbage???? That's right saints! He can't do it! He's pure, holy, righteous, and just and he just doesn't dwell in sin! He loves the sinner people, but he HATES SIN!

If you want victory in Jesus Christ, it comes with a heavy price, but it's a price that's worth paying in order to gain eternal life with Jesus...There so many people that are "prone.." to the prosperity message that when a preacher come in teaching and preaching holiness, repentance, and sanctification, people want to draw up, bow up, and be ready to fight...but I'm one preacher that isn't backing down from my purpose..

Without sanctification, (holiness) NO MAN shall see God...Yeah, you have territory, and yes, God wants to bless you, but I'm a firm believer that God will not bless you and you living any ole' kind of way!

I'm a young minister that don't know all the ropes of ministry, but I'm a believer in holiness and sanctification...and through all the things that I have been through in my life, God had to make me real!!!!!! I used to play church, I used to serve God for what he can give me, I used to have men up before God and then had my hand out for blessings...Oh, but through it all, God made me real!!!!!!! Total submission is required saints of God....you can't run from God! If he has a calling on your life, you can run, but you can't hide....allow God to do a work in you in order for you to go to the next level! The church was instilled in me from a child on up and there were young men that I called myself dating that tried to take me off that pathway...I would be strong for a little while, but eventually, they took me off the pathway because I had no root to keep me grounded in the Lord.

Your deliverance is not for you to keep to yourself...there are some people out in the world waiting on you to come and minister deliverance to them, and if you are lagging behind, still pleasing the flesh, still disgruntled over your present conditions, ect...then you are prolonging your own seasons!!!!!

"Therefore I glory in Christ Jesus in my service to God" (Romans 15:17).

"Jesus looked at them and said, 'With man this is impossible, but not with God; all things are possible with God'" (Mark 10:27).

"Now faith is being sure of what we hope for and certain of what we do not see" (Hebrews 11:1).

"We live by faith and not by sight" (2 Corinthians 5:7).

So your question for me may be asked something like this: How I embrace humility? That's a very simple question. Embracing humility isn't easy. To me, it's a process. When you are stripped from all resources that you have always depended in such as having a job, a home, a car to drive, a spouse, friends, resources ect it leaves you in a challenging predicament, but as a Child of God it's your choice to decide how you will deal with humility. You can either pray or ask God to help you through this and believe that there is a blessing in going through a wilderness experience, or you can be disgruntled and fight going through it. You can believe that he is going to work things out for the good as his word promised. Romans 8:28 says; and we know that all things work together for good to them that love God, to them who are the called according to his purpose. I believe that my trials and tribulations are preparing me for greater things that may come my way. I believe God is preparing me to be an effectual witness to those that I will minister to throughout my journey. I had too much trust in earthly people and too much trust in material things, and now that my resources are limited, I have learned how to lean and depend on God for all of my needs. I believe that it's a reason for going through this season, and humility humbles us. God has to get his glory and what better way to get it by taking his children through a season of humility where we will be stripped from resources, and tested to see how we will withstand trials and tribulations…God has to get his glory, for he shares it with no one. James 1:2-3 says; 2My brethren, count it all joy when ye fall into divers temptations; 3Knowing this, that the trying of your faith worketh patience. How does humility increases your anointing may be another question asked. To me, humility increases your anointing because first of all, God is getting his glory that's rightfully due to him. When you humble yourself, you will be exalted. Luke 14:11 says; For whosoever exalteth himself shall be abased; and he that humbleth himself shall be exalted. When you are humbled, your purpose for sharing the Gospel will not be to accumulate riches from preaching the Gospel. You will learn how to love and serve others instead of vice versa. Humility increases your anointing because God will get his glory that is rightfully due to him, he will not share it with you...You cannot take credit for what he does through you, for it's him that uses you. Who God bruises the most, he uses the most. Humility humbles you in order to be used by God. If you are not humbled, you had better humble yourself! Because one thing for sure, you don't want to ask God to do it, for when he do it, it will be not the way you expected it! So humble yourself.

"A Broken Spirit and a Contrite Heart"

The road before me pounding with rain,

If I continue to travel it, I will never be the same.

Sink holes keep throwing me around,

This time I won't quit, can't let anything slow me down...

Don't know the reason why I have to take this road,

But I trust God in it all, a story that must not go untold...

I've been broken and I need to be fixed again,

As the world around me don't understand...

That in order to be of much use,

I must be restored again, and not suffer through this abuse...

(for those that are just starting to heal from having your heart broken)

Lord make me whole again...*Shanetria*

Psalm 51:17 The sacrifices of God are a broken spirit: a broken and a contrite heart, O God, thou wilt not despise.

It has been nearly four years that my daughter was born. We have been through so much together and I thank God for providing for us. I walked around for a long while out of work, had to stop attending college because I refused to take out another student loan to help fund my education, (I'm already in debt), I still live with my parents, I do have a car, but I don't have my license, (don't have money for insurance), so everyday, I'm at home with my daughter, I rarely get to go any place other than occasional shopping and of course to church with my family. I'm in a very hard predicament and there are times where I get sad for I long for the load to be lightened just a little bit if possible, I'm learning how to see the light through all of this. God is taking me through a season of complete stripping of everything that I supposed gave me life, I'm learning to function without material things because those things will not have any part in what God wants to do through us.

God has been my source and my strength, I have acknowledged my call into the ministry, but haven't gotten the okay to go forward, so I minister by way of writing...I can encourage any of you single moms that's going through a storm to hang on in it and never let go of your faith in God, for he's the only one that will see us through it. I don't know what's going to happen in me and my daughter's life on tomorrow, or neither do I know about the future, but I do wake up every morning with hope that things will change for the both of us. Love and prayers to all of you and if no one has ever told you..."kudos to you for being so strong and not giving up in the struggle..."

It grieves my heart when I think about events that have taken place in my past. Something's we want to forget so we can heal and move on. Moving forward sometimes means: "We have to close the door on the past so that we can move on..."

Closing the door on past pain means:

*Never forgetting what happened or what the person or (persons) has done to cause pain to your emotions, but forgiving them for what transpired.

*Asking God to heal open bleeding wounds

*Forgiving yourself and moving on

*Cry it out if you have to. Crying does have a way of making you feel better!

*Read scriptures pertaining to hurt....

You may be depressed about the predicament past situations have placed you in such as: Being a single parent, limited income to support those kids, ect...

Psalm 3:3 But You, oh Lord, are a shield for me, my glory, and the lifter of my head.

Psalm 40:1-3 I waited patiently and expectently for the Lord; and He inclined to me and heard my cry. He drew me out of a horrible pit (a pit of tumult and of destruction), out of the miry clay (froth and slime), and set my feet upon a rock, steadying my steps and establishing my goings. And He has put a new song in my mouth, a song of praise to our God. Many shall see and fear (revere and worship) and put their trust and confident reliance in the Lord.

Isaiah 60:1 Arise (from the depression and prostration in which circumstances have kept you - rise to a new life)! Shine (be radiant with the glory of the Lord), for your light has come, and the glory of the Lord has risen upon you!
Psalm 31:7-8 I will be glad and rejoice in Your mercy and steadfast love, because You have seen my affliction, You have taken note of my life's distresses, and You have not given me into the hand of the enemy; You have set my feet in a broad place.

And finally............here is a prayer for depression that you can say over and over. Oh Lord, as I sit here in the middle of all my mess, I don't have much strength or energy to pray. But I'm lifting up my head and my eyes to you because I know deep in my heart that you have the power to do all things. I believe that you want me to be happy and healthy more than I do. And I know you have a good plan for my life.

God, as I bring you my pain, please direct it into something good. Please heal me. Your Word says that ALL things work together for good to those who love you and are called according to your purpose. Let my healing be a testimony to all the GREAT things you do every day.

I just raise my head to thank you Lord. Thank you for hearing me. Thank you for loving me enough to take care of me. And thank you for showing me what I need to do to feel better.

I ask and receive everything in Jesus' name. Amen! You may ask me the question how should I be strong while going through trials? You can't be strong in your own strength; you must rely on Jesus Christ to make you strong first and foremost. So much come at your way at one time and before you can get through one trial, another one pops up, but the joy of the Lord is your strength. Don't let trials and tribulations keep you from praising God. I have been going through a storm for four years now, although it's difficult at times, I get joy knowing that my trials and tribulations are momentarily. My strength comes from Jesus Christ. The hardest struggle that I'm going through is right now: When God gives you a promise, don't think that opposition will not come agaisnt it. I'm going through opposition but the joy of the Lord is my strength! I remember all of the time that I gave to the enemy to do my own thing, but now I give the Lord my whole entire life to do what he will in me. No matter how difficult things get for me, the joy of the LORD is my strength.

Psalm 121 says;

1I will lift up mine eyes unto the hills, from whence cometh my help.

2My help cometh from the LORD, which made heaven and earth.

3He will not suffer thy foot to be moved: he that keepeth thee will not slumber.

4Behold, he that keepeth Israel shall neither slumber nor sleep.

5The LORD is thy keeper: the LORD is thy shade upon thy right hand.

6The sun shall not smite thee by day, nor the moon by night.

7The LORD shall preserve thee from all evil: he shall preserve thy soul.

8The LORD shall preserve thy going out and thy coming in from this time forth, and even for evermore.

It's hard to look around you and see your family moving forward. It's hard and at times you may cry because things seem to be standing still. It's your responsibility to get a warrior attitude that no matter what may be going on around me, I'm going to embrace and weather my storm. Romans 8:35-39 says; 35Who shall separate us from the love of Christ? shall tribulation, or distress, or persecution, or famine, or nakedness, or peril, or sword? 36As it is written, For thy sake we are killed all the day long; we are accounted as sheep for the slaughter. 37Nay, in all these things we are more than conquerors through him that loved us.

38For I am persuaded, that neither death, nor life, nor angels, nor principalities, nor powers, nor things present, nor things to come, 39Nor height, nor depth, nor any other creature, shall be able to separate us from the love of God, which is in Christ Jesus our Lord. So you ask how I overcome temptations. From the depths of this soul a longing still hides,

I'm feeling overwhelmed, I swallow my pride. Waiting to still fill that empty void, I don't take matters in my hand, but I give it to the Lord for he completely understands. He's able to keep me in the deepest hour of temptation;

    I give it to him without a moment's hesitation. In the whispers of the night when I'm alone, I have to pray for God's grace to carry me on. Every part of me, I'm praying to be returned and to be caught up in bondage again, is not my desire, for life's lesson I have learned. Temptation is something that every Christian faces. There's not a one of us that struggle with temptation of some sort, but it's what we do when we are tempted that proves whether we rely on the strength of the Lord to carry us through or not. It's easy to shoot off excuses about the desires that are there, but Jesus requires us to rely on him for strength even in the hour of our deepest tempting and desires. As a Saved, Single, Christian young mother, I do have desires. What I do to overcome those desires is, I pray and ask God for strength. I often go to God's word for guidance and I rely on the Lord to sustain me in my tempting. It's extremely important to have an effective prayer life and to keep yourself in the presence of God.

Sometimes, you may do all this and still be overwhelmed with temptation, but I'm a firm believer that God will provide a way to escape. If you are struggling with temptation, here are some scriptures that will help you:

Temptation

"Your word I have treasured in my heart, that I may not sin against You."

Psalms 119:11

"He who conceals his transgressions will not prosper, but he who confesses and forsakes them will find compassion."

Proverbs 28:13

"For sin shall not be master over you, for you are not under law but under grace."

Romans 6:14

"Therefore let him who thinks he stands take heed that he does not fall. No temptation has overtaken you but such as is common to man; and God is faithful, who will not allow you to be tempted beyond what you are able, but with the temptation will provide the way of escape also, so that you will be able to endure it."

1 Corinthians 10:12, 13

"Finally, be strong in the Lord and in the strength of His might. Put on the full armor of God, so that you will be able to stand firm against the schemes of the devil. In addition to all, taking up the shield of faith with which you will be able to extinguish all the flaming arrows of the evil one."

Ephesians 6:10-11, 16

"For since He Himself was tempted in that which He has suffered, He is able to come to the aid of those who are tempted."

Hebrews 2:18

"Therefore, since we have a great high priest who has passed through the heavens, Jesus the Son of God, let us hold fast our confession. For we do not have a high priest who cannot sympathize with our weaknesses, but One who has been tempted in all things as we are, yet without sin. Therefore let us draw near with confidence to the throne of grace, so that we may receive mercy and find grace to help in time of need."

Hebrews 4:14-16

"Consider it all joy, my brethren, when you encounter various trials, knowing that the testing of your faith produces endurance. Blessed is a man who perseveres under trial; for once he has been approved, he will receive the crown of life which the Lord has promised to those who love Him."

James 1:2-3, 12

"Let no one say when he is tempted, I am being tempted by God; for God cannot be tempted by evil, and He Himself does not tempt anyone. But each one is tempted when he is carried away and enticed by his own lust."

James 1:13, 14

"Submit therefore to God. Resist the devil and he will flee from you."

James 4:7

"In this you greatly rejoice, even though now for a little while, if necessary, you have been distressed by various trials, so that the proof of your faith, being more precious than gold which is perishable, even though tested by fire, may be found to result in praise and glory and honor at the revelation of Jesus Christ."

1 Peter 1:6-7

"Be of sober spirit, be on the alert. Your adversary, the devil, prowls around like a roaring lion, seeking someone to devour. But resist him, firm in your faith, knowing that the same experiences of suffering are being accomplished by your brethren who are in the world."

1 Peter 5:8-9

"Then the Lord knows how to rescue the godly from temptation."

2 Peter 2:9a

"If we confess our sins, He is faithful and righteous to forgive us our sins and to cleanse us from all unrighteousness."

1 John 1:9

"You are from God, little children, and have overcome them; because greater is He who is in you than he who is in the world."

1 John 4:4

"Now to Him who is able to keep you from stumbling, and to make you stand in the presence of His glory blameless with great joy, to the only

God our Savior, through Jesus Christ our Lord, be glory, majesty."

Jude 24-25a

      I know how it feels when you feel as though you are walking all alone and that you're not thought or cared about but I send an encouraging word to you today that GOD CARES! Yes, GOD CARES! That's enough to put a smile on your face and dry your eyes. Someone may say today well, that's not enough reassurance, but let me tell you. If you CALL UPON HIM in true sincerity and have faith to KNOW that he will be there, he will come. Peace will fall all upon you and it's the best feeling in the world knowing that you are in the arms of Jesus. Most of us as Women of God are walking in singleness. Whether it's by choice, by circumstance, or just haven't found the right person yet. Whatever the case may be, God is looking for us to have total faith and dependency on him to guide us through. The word says that it was not good for man to be alone so he made HIM A SUITABLE HELPMEET. Believe God that he will bring that suitable helpmeet in his timing...minister God's word back to him!

      This is God's word. So when you lean on Jesus in total dependency, he will bring you a spouse in due season (if it's his will) the most important thing that we must do is seek HIS WILL. Because lonliness is a flesh situation and since it's a flesh situation, it's easy to do things in the flesh to try and fill that void. Jesus told us that he will never leave us nor forsake us and lo he is with us even until the end of the world. So that's a antedote for our lonliness. Masturbation, joining dating services, trying to go out before God and find a spouse isn't the answer. A man, sex, a desire for sex, ect...can't fill that void. I'm not sitting up here telling anyone that you won't get to a point in your singleness where you desire to have these things but this is the time that we should depend solely on the Lord. I'm too walking in your shoes and I too tell you that it's not easy all of the time. I get frustrated sometimes, at times I do wonder if I am forgotten about, but then the Lord always let me know that he is there walking beside me.

      The most important thing that we don't want to do is sin in our lonely state. Masturbation is a instrument of the Devil because it causes a man or woman to take what God created to be natural and use it against nature. That's why a person feels guilty afterwards...after the desired result is achieved, guilt sets in. Not only do you have loneliness to still combat but also guilt! As Christian single women and mothers, we must pray and ask God to help us. Lean and depend on him and ask his will to be done in our lives. God has a spouse for each one of us that he has chosen one for but are we willing to wait on God to present him to us? That's the question. Even if we have to wait eight years. Someone may say, "Well, that's too long!" "I can't wait that long.

"No, it's not too long." The word of God says, "WITH GOD ALL THINGS ARE POSSIBLE TO THOSE WHO BELIEVE." It's too long when we depend on the flesh to lead and guide us. Just because you are lonely doesn't mean that God is going to send Prince Charming on your doorstep tomorrow. So the thing that we must do is learn to be governed by our spirit and not by our flesh. I'm not saying that you won't fall, but a righteous man have the wisdom to get up, confess his or her sin to God, repent and keep moving. If you stay there and wallow, Satan will come and set more and more traps for the self-pity person. God don't want us walking around feeling sorry for ourselves. He wants us to walk around with joy in all things even when we fall beneath his will, he LOVES US! We must learn to confess, repent, and keep striving for righteousness.

Do not get caught up in the overwhelming feelings of that particular temptation. You have fought long and hard for your deliverance and when you are weak, Jesus will carry you through it if you rely on him to take you through. Yes, desires are present in my body, but do I think its okay to act on those desires even in thoughts? No I do not think its okay! We are to trust in Jesus for every mountain that is too hard and steep to climb. I'm focusing on honoring him in body mind and spirit which are his. I have paid a heavy price for my deliverance and I refuse to allow the enemy to enslave me in bondage again. The things that I'm going to share here, is for individuals who may be traveling down a similar pathway that I did previously. (It's for mature individuals) My desire is to help you and my deliverance is not for to keep for myself so here goes: How do you try to put on a smile when you are bleeding inside? Well, this is what I did every since I was a child...I was always a loner...I always was afraid....I hated loud noises and I hated when others raised their voices, but some kind of way, God gave me forbearance through others arguing and even fighting. I often dreamed of becoming a singer. I could sing really well, play the keyboard, write my own songs, and put the music to my songs, so as a teenager, I was always singing, and writing songs. That was one thing that I found comfort in. I also found comfort in writing stories and poetry. I never did believe that it would take me anywhere. I was a child with big DREAMS. I didn't know God like I know him now, but some kind of way, I always felt like I was his special child. My mouth would be stuck to the roof of my mouth when I was in the presence of arguing ...sometimes my head would pound, and silently I wished for a way out. My household wasn't perfect as I'm sure there are none that are. I often day-dreamed about leaving and following my dreams of singing and that got me through a lot of those years of pain. In this book, I will share with you real life events that I have went through...my hope and prayer is that you start thanking God with me for I could have been dead and sleeping in my grave, because I could have been found in a ditch somewhere thrown there by men after they had their pleasure with me, but it is only by God's grace and his grace alone, that I am still here to live and to tell other women in sexual bondage that, there is a way out. The devil want many of us to be silent on speaking on our deliverance from bondages that we were in at some time or another. By being "silent," that's his way of holding our past over our heads so that he can pick a later date to try and taunt us, but it's time for us to come out of our silence and help someone else who may be traveling down a similar pathway to destruction. I lost my virginity at age 16 and I discovered that it was very "painful..." and every since that day: September 10, 1996 I felt extremely guilty for losing something that was very precious to me. At age seventeen, I had my first encounter of a man not stopping when you tell him to "stop..." by my very own boyfriend. I had a lot of trust in him and never believed that he would do anything to hurt me. I know I had a little too much trust in him...I remember the day as though it happened yesterday. Part of this was my fault because I let it happened. I felt terribly horrified when I realized what he was doing to me. Finally, with all the strength that I could muster, I got away from him. I was shaken up and in haste I put my back clothes on. That was my first sexual tyranny account The reason why I say that it was my fault, was because I gave him access to my body instead of telling him "no," that I didn't want to have sex with him. After that horrible experience, I felt deprived and I did not desire to have a boyfriend for a long while after that. During the remainder of the summer of 1997, I began to get closer to God. I would listen to Gospel everyday, but soon my desires for men returned. I somehow stumbled through my teenaged years looking for love, searching for acceptance, trying to feel like I was apart of this world. When I was a young child all the way through my teenage years, I was very suicidal and didn't feel like I was a person. I often had thoughts of killing myself whether by drowning in the bathtub or by other means. Those thoughts were very heavy in my mind. I was extremely depressed, especially at age fifteen when I struggled with my eating disorder. I was always heavy set, I didn't feel like I was pretty although, I was told that I was…My hair was really long, and I had a pretty face, but somehow, I felt like I was never going to be accepted because of my weight. I searched far and wide trying to find what I needed in earthly men but all I found was disappointment and heartache. Confusion was escalading everywhere around me and the only refuge I found at the time was in men and sex. I was becoming well-known to the guys at my school. Being the pretty, heavy-sets shy girl, with the big boobs, I had many friends. I was sweet and most men took advantage of that particular fact. Most guys in my high school thought since I had big boobs, that I was easy and I got preyed on and taunted sexually because I had them. Sometimes, I was afraid to go to lunch and in certain areas where those guys hung out because I was afraid of being sexually assaulted. I didn't even have a desire to go to school. I was a good student and very well liked by all of my teachers but because of not wanting to face certain guys at my school, I didn't want to go. Being the victim of a sexual tyranny account, I often felt uneasy around certain guys. Right now to this day, I feel very uneasy around certain guys...when I pick up on those that harbor a womanizing spirit. In my younger days, the majority of the guys wanted to get with me but now for the reasons that I thought. One day at P.E. I was standing by the bleachers and one of my friend's saw something written on there that she wanted me to see. When I went to see what was written I felt like an invisible hand had just punched me in my chest. It had my name and underneath it was the statement: Good(you may fill in the blanks) at the time that was written, I had only been with one guy and that was my boyfriend who had took my virginity, when asked about it, he totally denied it and I was naive enough to believe him. I don't remember if I scribbled it out or if one of my friend's did, but after that encounter, I didn't care what any of them thought about me. I was going through a lot and the only refuge I found was in sex, but I was starting to feel extremely guilty, but I just didn't know who to talk to. It was horrible trying to fumble your way through with feelings that you couldn't share with anyone. Most of my feelings were shared with my grandmother. I remember opening the door one night and fleeing out in just my nightgown and no shoes on my feet to seek comfort in her arms. I was bleeding inside and I was searching for comfort...There was so much inside of me that I wanted to share but I couldn't. I was extremely afraid. In my teenage years, my grandmother was my biggest refuge and most things I shared with her, but the rest, I hid because I was afraid to tell others. This book is really hard for me to write and if it seems like I'm talking monosyllabic, it's not intended because I want to share only so much, and most things are just between me and God and I won't be able to share them with anyone else. I'm not worried about the condemnation that I may receive from others, because I have really became transparent before the Lord and my ministry is primarily to help those who are being silenced by the enemy about their past. Let me encourage you...stop worrying about what others will say and think about you...God is the only one that you are to please...he's the only one that you are living holy and upright for. Don't let people cause your ministry to stay within you....there's purpose and destiny in your womb that is waiting to come forth. Tell the devil he is a liar and that you are going to tell others where God have brought you from no matter what means you use, whether by book writing, song, holding seminars around the world to, whatever way God is leading you to minister, be obedient to him. This is not easy for me, but as I continue to write, I feel so much being released from me and that's a good thing for me...

By the age of twenty I was having sex and in and out of relationships with a few men that only used me for that purpose. I had started to not care about my reputation.

For a very long time I lived with guilt over the past sins that I have committed, but I'm so very glad that I can say today that guilt no longer has dominion over me. In the past I didn't realize that there were severe consequences that we reap when we walk and do things that are contrary to God's intended purpose. Like for instance:

- Having sex with numerous partners (STD's)
- Using Drugs (Overdose)
- Drinking Alcohol (Cirrhosis of the liver)
- Smoking Cigarettes (lung cancer)

and the list goes on...our bodies are precious and they are the temple of the Holy Ghost. That's why it bothers me so when people say that they are born again, but yet and still, they do things that are harmful to their bodies...they still please their temples. Something is wrong somewhere, because the Holy Ghost cannot and will not dwell in an unclean temple! Deliverance is extremely important...because without it, sin will constantly have dominion over your life causing severe guilt. Un-confessed sin will cause the devil to keep you enslaved in bondage.

> I thank the Lord because I could have got Aids and passed it on to my daughter! That could be me dying of cancer! That could have been me fighting for my life on a hospital bed, I could have been dead sleeping in my grave, but it's by the grace of God that I am here, and I'm going to continue thanking and praising God for bringing me through dangers seen and unseen! It's by his grace that I'm still growing strong and doing the work that he has ordained for me to do! I pray the words placed here will help somebody not only am I sharing my testimony, but I am ministering to the bound captives who are afraid to come out and walk with God. I am a walking and living testimony! If you continue to dip and dab in sin and don't stop abusing your temples, your sins will and can catch up with you! HIV/AIDS is not playing with a living soul! Abusing your temples will catch up with you in the long run. That's why when you come in the knowledge

of Christ, you should now be walking in his ways and his statues, you should be walking in the newness of life. No longer should you stay walking in the old way that you used to. There should be a change in you! If any man be in Christ, he is a new creature, old things have passed away and behold all thing are brand new! Not just some things, but all things! I thank God that I can stand in the gap for those who have not received their deliverance as of yet. I thank God for adequately preparing me to minister healing and deliverance to other youth and young adults who are on drugs, prostituting their bodies, those suffering from severe depression and rejection, those who are living with HIV/Aids, those that society and even the church reject. Many people may say that the church shouldn't accept sinners but if the body of Christ doesn't accept them then who will? Deliverance is an ongoing process just as well as being instructed in the ways and principles of God...Spiritual growth takes time...and it's not going to happen overnight! It got some hurting and wounded people out there, and if we don't know how to minister to their needs, they are not going to stay in the church...that's just as simple as it get. We weren't saved all of our lives, so we need to be considerate of those that are trying to grow in the knowledge of God's word. It's a major difference between a person that's trying than a person that is using the church when things are not going the way they want them to go, but when things are going good, they go back out in the world of sin. God helps those that want to be helped. I thank God for straightening me out, cleansing me, and filling me with his precious holy ghost...now that I'm on the right road, I thank God that I can go out there and help others to the right road.

Christians must learn to WAIT! Wait I say on the Lord! Isaiah 40:31 [AMP] says; But those who wait for the Lord [who expect, look for, and hope in Him] shall change and renew their strength and power; they shall lift their wings and mount up [close to God] as eagles [mount up to the sun]; they shall run and not be weary, they shall walk and not faint or become tired.(A)

We are to be examples to the world on how to be patient and wait! It's sad when Christians don't know how to wait on God but instead lean to their own understanding and try to go out before God's timing and do things on their own. It's even more alarming to see many Christians who think they can change someone. Jesus is the only one that does the changing in us. He didn't put anyone of us down here to do a change in someone. Many of us are standing in the way or hindering someone else from receiving their deliverance and from being in the place that God has ordained for them failing to realize that God will get them to where they need to be eventually! Remember he has a plan!

Many of us are ministers of the Gospel but don't know who we are CALLED TO! We are not called to minister to everyone...God has a specific people that we are called to. People are really not getting this and in turn they are getting frustrated when things don't seem to click together in their ministry. We must pray and ask God to lead us to the person or persons that we are to called to!

Hmmm..Doesn't this also include relationships? The word of God tells us in Matthew 19:5-6;

5And said, For this reason a man shall leave **his** father and mother and shall be united firmly (joined inseparably) **to his wife**, and the two shall become one flesh?(A)

This verse doesn't say leave his father and mother and be united firmly to **A WIFE but HIS WIFE!**

19:6 So they are no longer two, but one flesh. **What therefore God has joined together, let not man put asunder (separate).**

There are millions of men and women in the world today but we are not called to ALL OF THEM. God ordaines and choose a special SOMEONE for each individual who are willing to be PATIENT AND WAIT FOR THAT PERSON! That's why the divorce rate is so high even among Christians and it's because we are not willing to wait on God! WE want what we want and we want who we want failing to realize that just because we want it doesn't mean that God has to conform to it! He knew who would coincide with your anointing before he even formed you! Yesterday I mentioned that we have a birthdate and a death date and in between that time frame has already been ordained. I don't care how we try to make and stick something together, what happens between that timeline has already been but do we have the discipline to figure that out and line up with God's will for our lives?

There's no need to get mad, upset, or even try to do things to try and keep a man or a woman! If they are not simply for you, they are just not for you. God keeps letting me know that his will shall be done regardless of what the situation look like and regardless of who try to stand between what he has already ordained. If it's meant to be it's meant to be and there's no human that can **CHANGE THAT!** Praise the Lord! The question I'm asking today is: Are you willing to wait for it? Are you willing to prepare for it? Are you willing to stand for it even when others say: "It will never happen." This goes for anything in life and not just relationships...what visions and dreams do you have for yourself? What talents have God placed in your hands? Are you willing to develop it? Are you willing to wait for them to grow and develop when everyone around you screams that it will never happen?

I'm learning in this life that if **GOD BE FOR ME** who can be against me? I don't care what is said about me or what is thought about me....people get upset and angry because you choose to stand firm on God's will for your life and that the person or persons that they are desiring are ordained for **YOU or that you are anointed to operate in a calling they they are desiring!** Yes, I'm standing firmly for my blessing because God gave it to me and I'm willing to wait for it to come to past! I'm praying for it and I'm believing God for it because what GOD HAS FOR ME, it is for me and **THE BLESSING** is mines. I don't care what Devil try to obtain what's mine illegally, **THERE'S NO WEAPON FORMED AGAINST ME THAT SHALL PROSPER...**Many people right now in relationships with a person or persons that God has ordained for someone else and they are wondering why the relationship is not going as planned. God has a person fit especially for who you are and what you are designed to become and if that person doesn't fit your character, you **CAN'T CHANGE THEM TO FIT WHO YOU ARE!** God is the changer and the rearranger...sadly people will have to find this the hard way because they are choosing to stand in places that God has not ordained for them so whatever we face not being in the will of God, we bring consequences on ourselves!

Reminder: Something's that God reveals to us is not to be shared in this designated season! I have to get reminded of this over and over again...Know when and what to share and what to be silent on...

 and there are some that's trying to make future events happen today instead of the designated time, season, and place that God has appointed for it to happen. There are many distractions that have taken place over the course of the last few months. The devil is catching Christians off guard left and right, but it's time now dear siblings to get back in line with God's word! To anyone out there tonight who may be reading this book that may be in a backslidden condition, I beg you to get back in line with God and hurry! There's too much idling going on, too much gossiping, scandalizing others names, and speaking falsely of others going on. If we know a person that is struggling spiritually in the body of Christ, it's our responsibility to pray for them, encourage them, and lift them up instead of putting them down, talking about them, and tearing them down. We are to Be helpers of one another. God used the time away to show me some things. During this time he showed me how to speak the truth in love. There's a boundary between ministering to others out of love and **condemning.**

Seeing the conditions of the church, does have a tendency to vex us, but we can't let the condition of it cause us to get in the flesh and judge it!

Our job is to do what God has instructed us to do…as ministers of the Gospel, our responsibility is to share God's word with others, love them, pray for them, and encourage them. Our job is not to make anyone live for God. We must learn when and how to draw boundaries. We share God's word, the word draws them, and God does the converting. It's easy to run from things when the burden seems to get heavy, but if God is telling us to stay there and trust him through whatever burden we are facing on behalf of ministering to God's people, we are to be obedient to him, and stand firm on God's word no matter what. Yes, the church is in chaos, yes, there are many things that we need to do before Jesus returns, but what are we doing about it? Are we praying for the condition of the church to improve or are we too busy pointing out what the church isn't doing? I don't believe in compromising and sugarcoating, I believe in letting the Lord have his way in my life. I'm not going to lose my soul to Satan to burn in a burning hell for not doing what the Lord has chosen and ordained me to do. The Lord has sent me on here to continue to warn in love! Each one of us has a role and a responsibility to carry out for God. Love is not an obligation, for if you are Holy Ghost filled, and born-again, love should automatically flow out of your heart because God IS love!

1 Corinthians 13

1 Though I speak with the tongues of men and of angels, and have not charity, I am become as sounding brass, or a tinkling cymbal.

2 And though I have the gift of prophecy, and understand all mysteries, and all knowledge; and though I have all faith, so that I could remove mountains, and have not charity, I am nothing.

3 And though I bestow all my goods to feed the poor, and though I give my body to be burned, and have not charity, it profiteth me nothing.

4Charity suffereth long, and is kind; charity envieth not; charity vaunteth not itself, is not puffed up,

5Doth not behave itself unseemly, seeketh not her own, is not easily provoked, thinketh no evil;

6Rejoiceth not in iniquity, but rejoiceth in the truth;

7Beareth all things, believeth all things, hopeth all things, endureth all things.

8Charity never faileth: but whether there be prophecies, they shall fail; whether there be tongues, they shall cease; whether there be knowledge, it shall vanish away.

9For we know in part, and we prophesy in part.

10But when that which is perfect is come, then that which is in part shall be done away.

11When I was a child, I spake as a child, I understood as a child, I thought as a child: but when I became a man, I put away childish things.

12For now we see through a glass, darkly; but then face to face: now I know in part; but then shall I know even as also I am known.

13And now abideth faith, hope, charity, these three; but the greatest of these is charity.

I'm not concerned about hear-say. I'm not concerned about what others may have said or is currently saying behind my back, I'm not concerned about seeking riches, houses, and land. I'm not concerned about what I don't have...but I AM concerned about my soul and where it will spend eternity. I'm working out my own soul's salvation with fear and trembling. I'm not serving God because I fear consequences of not serving him. I serve him because as a born again Christian, that's my REASONABLE SERVICE....that desire, was automatically birthed in my heart when I received the Holy Ghost. It's not an obligation or a duty. I thank God for blessing me little by little. I thank him for my child, my future husband, his child, and my family. I'm not consuming my time worrying about what's going to happen in the future, getting consumed with a relationship, act...but what I am consumed with is serving and being obedient to God.

One thing we all know about fire and that is it is hot! But one thing we know that water can do, and that's put a fire out! Anytime we stop seeking God, anytime we stop trusting God, anytime we start seeking to do our will instead of God's will, anytime we start putting others before God, anytime we start worrying about our flesh instead of our spirit....look out, because trouble will come! The main problem that the church has is it doesn't know the difference between the flesh and the spirit...there's not a boundary drawn there.... (speak Holy Ghost) there are still people who are still focusing on things in the flesh instead of the spirit. The minute the pastor get up and preach a convicting sermon on Sunday, the first thought comes to mind of a person in the flesh is that, somebody must have told him/her something, failing to realize that God reveals things to his prophets as well as speak through them....they haven't grasped the concept that the flesh and the spirit is contrary the one to the other so that they cannot do the things that they would. They hadn't grasped the concept that if they will decrease and allow the Lord to increase, they will begin to see God move in their lives, speak to them, and their ears will become open in order to hear!

Galatians 5:16This I say then, Walk in the Spirit, and ye shall not fulfill the lust of the flesh.

For the flesh lusteth against the Spirit, and the Spirit against the flesh: and these are contrary the one to the other: so that ye cannot do the things that ye would.

18But if ye be led of the Spirit, ye are not under the law.

19Now the works of the flesh are manifest, which are these; Adultery, fornication, uncleanness, lasciviousness,

20 Idolatry, witchcraft, hatred, variance, emulations, wrath, strife, seditions, heresies,

21 Envyings, murders, drunkenness, revellings, and such like: of the which I tell you before, as I have also told you in time past, that they which do such things shall not inherit the kingdom of God.

22 But the fruit of the Spirit is love, joy, peace, longsuffering, gentleness, goodness, faith,

23 Meekness, temperance: against such there is no law.

24 And they that are Christ's have crucified the flesh with the affections and lusts.

25 If we live in the Spirit, let us also walk in the Spirit.

Glory to God! that last verse should make a light bulb come on in our head! If we live in the spirit, let us also walk in the spirit....that's in conversation, in actions, in deeds, in mind, in body, and in spirit. We should no longer take pleasure in pleasing our flesh...daily we are to be stripping from this flesh and putting on the likeness of Christ.

Instead of us talking about what the church is lacking, or judging the conditions of it, let us that are living for God, come together on one accord and began to pray for the church. Wouldn't it feel so much better while we are calling it to the attention of God's people, start bringing it to God in prayer instead of judging and condemning it? {Note* As a born again believer, the church is in "you."} Praise the Lord Saints of God. It's truly a blessing to be able to minister to you through this book. I believe in letting God have his way in my writings, so I'm going to place here whatever he places in my spirit.

Singles, you have been distracted long enough. God is getting ready to bless and pour out his blessings on his (true) children. There are a few of you that are not in place to receive all that God has for you. (Especially those that are seeking spouses)... Those that have been laboring, fasting, and being obedient to God, continue to labor in the spirit. Continue to cry aloud and spare not and help those that need to surrender themselves wholly to God. This entry tonight is primarily for single people.

The enemy is totally going about devouring those in the body of Christ that are distracted: That is: Worrying about who their spouse is going to be, searching for that spouse, placing ads on dating services, and constantly praying and crying out for God to give them a spouse. This behavior has distracted many Christian singles from their purpose. What are you doing in your season of singleness? *Are* you getting closer to God or *do you desire* something that you don't have permission to have right now?

This is a prophetic word that the Lord gave to me at the first part of the year concerning singles: (I'm going to put part of that word here)...

I hear the spirit saying...* Single Christian men and women have began to wish and long for husbands/wives, their pursuit of finding a husband/wife has taken precedence over their pursuit for finding and maintaining their relationship with Christ. *

God knew each one of us even before we were formed in our mother's womb. He knew if you would marry, and if you wouldn't marry.....he knows everything about every one of us....there's no need for any of us to beg for something that God may or may not have ordained for us.

Jeremiah 1:5

Before I formed thee in the belly I knew thee; and before thou camest forth out of the womb I sanctified thee, and I ordained thee a prophet unto the nations.

2 Timothy 3:1-7 Paul said, "In the last days perilous times shall come. For people shall be lovers of their own selves...unthankful, unholy, without natural affection....despisers of those that are good...lovers of pleasure more than lovers of God; having a form of Godliness but denying the

power thereof; from such turn away. For of this sort are they which creep into houses, and lead captive silly women laden with sins, led away by various lusts. Ever learning and never able to come to knowledge of the truth."

This is part of what the Lord revealed to me to give to Christian singles. It's easy to get caught up in wanting a spouse, but are you praying and asking God to adequately prepare you and that possible future spouse for marriage? Have you sought God on whether he wants you to be married or single?

Many people look around them and see their family and friends marry so their apprehension of wanting this same thing increases, but what about using this time to learning about becoming the Christian husband or that Christian wife that God wants you to be before the wedding bells ring?

Many people want to marry for reasons that are clearly not the (right) reasons.

1. **To satisfy sexual desires**
2. **To just have a husband or a wife**
3. **Family and friends are marrying**
4. **Wanting to have a child.... (Biological clock is ticking)**

5. To be supported financially

6. To give your child a father

There are other reasons why people want to rush marriage, but I listed only six. The above reasons are very selfish reasons for marriage. The union of marriage is not to be entered into lightly or discreetly. Surely if a person does not have anything to offer themselves, they will not have anything to offer a spouse either. Many people (women in general), sit around fantasizing about marriage, and they even pre-plan their weddings out! I'm not saying that anything is wrong with this, but what about taking the time that you are single or either courting and ask God to teach you how to become the wife that he needs you to be. (Vice versa men).

Anxiety and impatience can cause reckless behavior. This is not the attitude that a Christian should have.

Psalm 37:4 Delight thyself also in the LORD: and he shall give thee the desires of thine heart.

Psalm 37:5 Commit thy way unto the LORD; trust also in him; and he shall bring it to pass.

Psalm 37:6 And he shall bring forth thy righteousness as the light, and thy judgment as the noonday.

Psalm 37:7**(a)** Rest in the LORD, and wait patiently for him:

Psalm 127:2 It is vain for you to rise up early, to sit up late, to eat the bread of sorrows: for so he giveth his beloved sleep.

Matthew 6:25-34

Therefore I say unto you, Take no thought for your life, what ye shall eat, or what ye shall drink; nor yet for your body, what ye shall put on. Is not the life more than meat, and the body than raiment?

26Behold the fowls of the air: for they sow not, neither do they reap, nor gather into barns; yet your heavenly Father feedeth them. Are ye not much better than they?

27Which of you by taking thought can add one cubit unto his stature?

28And why take ye thought for raiment? Consider the lilies of the field, how they grow; they toil not, neither do they spin:

29And yet I say unto you, That even Solomon in all his glory was not arrayed like one of these.

30Wherefore, if God so clothe the grass of the field, which to day is, and to morrow is cast into the oven, shall he not much more clothe you, O ye of little faith?

31Therefore take no thought, saying, What shall we eat? or, What shall we drink? or, Wherewithal shall we be clothed?

32(For after all these things do the Gentiles seek:) for your heavenly Father knoweth that ye have need of all these things.

33But seek ye first the kingdom of God, and his righteousness; and all these things shall be added unto you.

34Take therefore no thought for the morrow: for the morrow shall take thought for the things of itself. Sufficient unto the day is the evil thereof.

"James, a servant of God and of the Lord Jesus Christ, to the twelve tribes which are scattered abroad, greeting. My brethren, count it all joy when ye fall into divers temptations; knowing this, that the trying of your faith worketh patience. But let patience have her perfect work, that ye may be perfect and entire, wanting nothing. If any of you lack wisdom, let him ask of God, that giveth to all men liberally, and upbraideth not; and it shall be given him."—James 1:1-5

(For those courting)

Preparation time for marriage is essential. Allow God to expose areas in your life that need to be worked on now before marriage is even thought about! Sitting around wishing, hoping, and longing, will not make God move any faster. So while you're waiting for your wedding day, you can also include marriage preparation individually as part of the wedding planning process.

Don't assume that you know what's best for you. Don't go out there and search for a mate. Allow God to prepare and bring the person that he has for you to be with. I will repeat this: "Allow God to prepare and bring the person that he has for you to be with." Stop assuming that your best is God's best. Seek him diligently and allow him to present you with the spouse that he has for you. I will pray for you...

Dear Father, there are many singles that are desperately wanting spouses. Lord help them to stop desiring, wishing, and longing for one, but instead seek your will concerning marriage. Help them to use their singleness to seek you instead of wishing to be married. IF you have revealed to them or have presented them with a mate, help them to understand that your desire is for them to wait until marriage before committing any sexual activity. Lord I pray for them to get back on track with you dear Father so that they can hear from you and carry out your commands for them to perform. Help them to realize that in their season of singleness that you want to shape and mold them into a presentable vessel for a spouse. Help them to realize if they are distracted, it will cause them to miss what you are trying to show them. Lord I ask for you to regulate their minds and their hearts, and if you have a spouse for them, you will present him (or) her to them in your given time. I ask all of these blessings in Jesus most precious name I pray. Amen, amen, and amen.

Don't You Know?

Your body is the temple of the Holy Ghost, which temple are ye?

It saddens my heart to see "professing" Christian single men" and "women" lusting after one another and God forbid, committing fornication and adultery...not just physically, but also mentally. hmmmm....does someone need deliverance?

The word of God says in Ephesians Chapter 5:1-3 says;

Be ye therefore followers of God, as dear children;

And walk in love, as Christ also hath loved us, and hath given himself for us an offering and a sacrifice to God for a sweetsmelling savour.

But fornication, and all uncleanness, or covetousness, let it not be once named among you, as becometh saints.

All of Ephesians 5 have some wonderful pointers for those who are born again Christians. It list things that we are not to be partakers of as becoming saints.

It's sad to see that so called born again Christians are bringing lust in the church.

It's sad to see some preachers with a wife in the congregation and a mistress also in the crowd.

It got women coming to church with everything that God gave them hanging out...Christian women that have husbands, you better watch some of these women smiling and grinning all in your face, because some of those same ones may be trying to seduce your husband on the slick. I'm not telling you something I heard, but something that I know. Watch these lusting demons!

God is dead tired of sin being brought in the church. He's dead tired of people that won't admit that they are in need of deliverance. They are not being delivered because they won't admit that they have a problem! Lust is a problem! It's not okay to lust...people that are dealing with lust, stop shooting off excuses to continue in your lust!

Let's move forward with the scriptures that the HolyGhost is giving to me to post here:

Ephesians 5:5-6 For this ye know, that no whoremonger, nor unclean person, nor covetous man, who is an idolater, hath any inheritance in the kingdom of Christ and of God.

6Let no man deceive you with vain words: for because of these things cometh the wrath of God upon the children of disobedience.

There's so much deception going on right in the church! You can expect deception from folk in the world, lusting from folk in the world, and sin from folk in the world, but when you have it going on in the church with men and women who get up and shout the church down on Sunday's, preaching, singing, and dancing until heaven get the news....then that's how you know the church got a problem....

What's wrong? It isn't God that got the problem, he's holy, just, righteous and pure....the finger pointing doesn't need to go to God or anyone else. Some people say well because Adam and Eve sinned, that's why I do." Yeah, they are the reason that sin was born in the world, but don't use that as an excuse to remain filthy! The problem is that there are some people that still have not died to the flesh, and if you are still struggling with sins in the flesh, there's no need to blame others, the problem is with Y-O-U!

Lust doesn't just define a sexual desire that goes for lusting after riches, lusting for power; ect... lust is a strong intense or unrestrained craving and desire.

I am talking about sexual lust since that's one of the basic problems that the church is facing today...if you don't believe me think about the priests that are molesting young boys, think about the ministers that are getting women pregnant, but already have wives and families... think about homosexuals and lesbians preaching the Gospel, in the choir stand, and on the pianos and keyboards...Lust is truly a factor that the church needs to deal with head on...because when you have leaders that can't control their flesh, then the whole congregation will suffer...

Ministers are word carriers...and Pastors are men after God's own heart...he is the one that shepherd's and oversees the flock. The mysteries of God's word is revealed to the Pastor so that he can feed the flock, some things are not revealed to the body, but instead may be revealed to the pastor so that he can reveal it to the body of Christ.

(When I say he that includes women Pastors too)...

If you are born-again, you should know how to carry yourself. You should know how to conduct yourselves. You should know what's off limits to you as becoming saints. The Internet is destroying many Christian's lives. Pornography is one of the factors that are destroying our Christian men.

It's a problem and the church body that can get a prayer through need to bring it to God in prayer! Many people are coming on this Internet living totally different lives than what they do in reality...they are using this tool to prey on innocent women and men, innocent children,ect...many, many, many, women are being deceived by the men that come on here pretending to be something they know that aren't!

That's why a Christian single woman, (especially) Christian single mothers, should precede online with caution. Also, there are some Christian married women getting caught up in the web of the Internet....sharing information with wolves in sheep's clothing and feelings start developing and pretty soon, a desire to be with that person. The devil knows that lust is a major factor and that's why he setting up traps for Christians to fall in! It's time to repent and go back to the way of the cross!

James 4:1 - 1From whence come wars and fighting's among you? come they not hence, even of your lusts that war in your members?

James 4:2 - Ye lust, and have not: ye kill, and desire to have, and cannot obtain: ye fight and war, yet ye have not, because ye ask not.

James 4:3 - Ye ask, and receive not, because ye ask amiss, that ye may consume it upon your lusts.

James 4:4 - Ye adulterers and adulteresses, know ye not that the friendship of the world is enmity with God? whosoever therefore will be a friend of the world is the enemy of God.

James 1:13 - Let no man say when he is tempted, I am tempted of God: for God cannot be tempted with evil, neither tempteth he any man:

Matthew 5:27 - Ye have heard that it was said by them of old time, Thou shalt not commit adultery:

Matthew 5:28 - But I say unto you, That whosoever looketh on a woman to lust after her hath committed adultery with her already in his heart.

Proverbs 6:25 - Lust not after her beauty in thine heart; neither let her take thee with her eyelids.

1 Peter 2:11 - Dearly beloved, I beseech you as strangers and pilgrims, abstain from fleshly lusts, which war against the soul;

Titus 3:3 - For we ourselves also were sometimes foolish, disobedient, deceived, serving divers lusts and pleasures, living in malice and envy, hateful, and hating one another.

Titus 3:4 - But after that the kindness and love of God our Saviour toward man appeared,

Titus 3:5 - 5Not by works of righteousness which we have done, but according to his mercy he saved us, by the washing of regeneration, and renewing of the Holy Ghost;

Women, when a man tells you that lusting after a woman isn't wrong, you tell him, well Jesus said in Matthew 5:28 says; "But, I say to you that whosoever looketh on a woman to lust after her, hath committed adultery with her already in his heart.

Putting the word on the devil will make him flee! James 4:7 says; Submit yourselves therefore to God. Resist the devil, and he will flee from you.

Christian men, (single men especially) if you are having problem with lust, then you need to take that problem to God and ask him to deliver you and set you free from it. You are the head and not the tail, above and not beneath. There are some sincere Christian sisters out there and not all of them are looking for sex and a good time, so just because you want sex, don't come on to a woman expecting that she does to.

Christian men with good intentions, not ALL women want just one thing. Allow God to give you his best. Most of you don't get encouraged, but I want to encourage you tonight to keep allowing God to lead you...ask him to teach you how to become a father to your children if you don't know how, and ask him to teach you how to govern your household if you feel that it's too much for you to handle.

Christian women, (single women especially) you are more than a bedroom partner. You are marriage material. Don't carry yourself in an unkempt way, for if you do, you will attract a wolf in sheep's clothing. You deserve to be treated with dignity and respect...and in order to have a fulfilling relationship, go back to Jesus your first love and be satisfied with him alone and when the time is right, if its his will, he will bring you his best... (a man after his own heart). A man will not respect you if you don't respect yourself.

Stop saying there are not any good Christian single men out there, because there are! If you allow God to give you his best, you will find the person that God had ordained for your life all alone. Don't go out there searching for him, let him find you! Stop talking about what Christian single men aren't and start praying for God to do a mighty work in them. God is going to use some of you to help him discover what he didn't even know what he possessed inside of him! Don't think you're going to get perfection. Expect to get someone that can be helped and that can help you! For whatever he's lacking spiritually, you are to pray for what he's lacking for God to do a work in him. You may be used as an instrument for his deliverance. Saints, let's not continue to allow lust to destroy the church's image. Let's pull together on one accord and fight the adversary and destroy his strongholds in the name of Jesus! When I didn't wait on God, I got what I attracted and it was always someone that was the opposite of who I was trying to be. I remember clearly one night me and my baby's father was at work. As a matter of a fact, it was my last night at my old job. He called me around 9:30 p.m. (we rode to work together)...and since I didn't have a car, he was my way around to everywhere that I had to go. He called me and told me that his son had a seizure and that he was on his way to the hospital.

We got off at ten o' clock originally so I was under the impression that he was coming to get me so we could ride to the hospital together. Well, when I asked him he told me that he didn't have any time to stop and come and pick me up on my building but to get someone else to drop me off at Rapides General. So me being naiive at the time,(but at the back of my mind, I was a bit suspicious). I believed him and I got a woman on our building to take me to the hospital. I remember her telling me to be careful and just talking to me on the way to the hospital. I didn't really want to hear anything anyone had to say about my baby's daddy not doing right by me. When we made it to the hospital, we hugged each other, and I got out of the car and went inside. I went to the check in desk and asked for my baby's father's son...I gave the clerk the name and she skimmed through the computer and told me: "I'm sorry but there's no one here by that name." I was so shocked! I asked her to try again...she went through the computer once again and repeated almost with an attitude: "I'm sorry there's no one here by that name." By that time the whole ER room was looking at me standing there in my work clothes uncertain of what to do. So I walked outside and walked all the way to the main part of the hospital to use a pay phone to call a taxi cab. I had to wait for nearly forty-five mintues for the cab to show up. Instead of me going home where I should have went, (my paretns live fifteen minutes from the hospital), I asked the cab driver to take me back to my baby's father's home (big mistake)...once there, I got out of my work clothing and made some phone calls. I called back up to Rapides General to ask for my baby's father's sister that worked there at the time. I told her what happend, so she went and checked the computer herself and came back and confirmed what the receptionist had told me. His son wasn't there. All throughout the night, she was calling me asking me had he called or come home and I told her no. She called the other two hospitals and that name was not registered at any of them. I couldn't believe this man had done this to me. So the next morning, his sister decided that she was going to come pick me up and we were going to ride around town and check at every probable place that he may have went. I was so mad at that time. I had murder on my mind. I'm not going to sit here and lie to any of you. I had "murder" on my mind. I wasn't at my self. My parents noticed a total change in my appearance. I have always had a pretty complexion because I have Indian on both sides of my family. But, I'm here to tell you today, I had to buy makeup a darker shade at that particular time in my life...something that I had never had to do. I relied on him to cook my food but I had stopped eating from him as time went on and he BEGAN TO NOTICE that I wasn't eating any of his food. Now, when people notice that you are not eating their cooking and they get upset, be suspicious! My parents had noticed how dark I had become...I didn't even seem like myself...I was almost to the point of violence in my behavior. I was indeed acting DEMONIC! You may think this is a game, but this is reality. Un-godly soul-ties are demonic and they will have you behaving in a way that you wouldn't morally behave! At that time I wanted to kill him for what he was putting me through, but now today I can say, this wasn't something that he put me through, this was something I put myself through because HE WAS NOT GOD'S WILL FOR MY LIFE! I laid a hammer on the counter by the door as I waited on his sister to come and pick me up. I wrote him a letter just in case he came home. I had in my mind that if he would have walked through that door that I was going to hit him in the head with that hammer. I took purex and I poured it in his open beer cans in the ice box, but after realization set in, I took those cans of beer and threw them in the trash. I couldn't do anything but just listen at the prompting of God letting me know that he wasn't worth going to jail behind. I was so devestated at the thought of killing him. Right now today, I couldn't believe that I had wanted to take someone else's life...If I had let the Devil have his way, I would be behind bars for my parents to raise my child.

His sister came and got me, and we rode around Alexandria after having breakfast and we didn't find him anywhere. By the time that we came back, I noticed that he had been home...he got my note because it was no longer in its spot...somehow I believed that he knew that I had violence on my mind. After awhile, he pulled up in the driveway, but when he saw me peep out the window, he quickly drove off again because he knew he was about to face a storm but he didn't realize how bad it was going to be. He didn't return home anymore that day, but would send word by his mom who was calling all day long telling me that he said he would be home later. His mom was telling me: "Don't leave my son." "Don't hurt my son." When he did come home, I didn't hurt him, but I hollered at him...I didn't make him forget what he had done to me. It didn't help because later on that night, he went out again. We argued, but he still left. After he left out of the house, I threw a shoe behind the door...it didn't do any good because he didn't come back home that night. I told this portion of my testimony to say this: "I don't care what you do if a man is not God's will for your life, it will not be!" This man was doing this I feel to try to keep me there with him. I would have clothes come up missing...and I felt that he was putting things in my food. At the time I suspected that I was pregnant (somehow he knew), but he didn't want another child...so I suspected that he was putting things in my food to make me get rid of my baby. At that time, I was going through morning sickness and feeling queasy so I didn't even desire to eat anything at that time anyway. I told this part of my testimony for those that are in abusive situations, those that are in situations where you KNOW God isn't present. Killing your spouse isn't worth it, although the Devil would put that thought in your mind. If you have kids, it's best to leave the situation when you can! If you find a way out of that predicament, GET OUT! To avoid having to hurt him to defend you and your children, get out of the situation! Why not listen to God in the first place so in that way you won't have to sit behind bars thinking back over what you should have done and the steps that you should have taken? What's not God's will, it's simply not God's will! I don't care what you try to do to make it work, if it's not what God said, IT SHALL NOT BE!

Poems

A Poem to God

As I close my eyes and drift to sleep, I pray the Lord my soul to keep.
In the dark of the night, where the turbulent waves keep out the light.
At a time like this while in despair, I lay my burdens on the altar and leave them there. It's hard to walk without finding the way, when you can't even tell the night from the day...
Trying to keep my head from hanging low,

but's it's hard when life keeps throwing a hard blow. I need you Lord right away, in this crazy world, I just can't stay...Take my hand and let me stand; let's walk through this hand in hand.

Stability and comfort do I see, but I know on earth it's not mines to keep, but in heaven, I will have the peace, that you have promised to me. One day I will leave this world and let it be...

I'm Bearing My Cross

See the nails driven in my hands,

With the blood dripping down to the sand.

The cross that I carry is heavy from hurt,

And from people treating me like dirt.

The cross that I carry bears guilt and shame,

And I have myself to blame.

But, I'm struggling on to Calvary's hill,

With dirt smudged on my face, mixed with tears...

Through the night, I battle with secrets of my past,

I hear the voice of Jesus calling to me at last...

No one knows the story that I have to tell,

Only I can tell it very well.

I'm learning now that most people I come into contact with is false,

But I'm learning a lesson now as I bear my cross.

The Greatest Part of Me

In between my timeline is where my life takes place,

I have a birthday and a death date...

I have had some good times, and some bad...

Some happy times and then some sad...

The worse part of my life is when I didn't know I lived...

If I could do it all again, my all I would give...

It wasn't until I knew,

That I had a Savior that loved me so dear and true...

I searched this earth far and wide,

But I couldn't find what I was seeking, no matter how I tried...

It wasn't until I discovered Jesus' love...

Unconditional love that streamed from above...

My heart wasn't a doormat that he just stepped on...

But he took it and fixed what was wrong...

I never knew happiness, no didn't know it could be...

Until I found the greatest part of me…

Shania

Her beautiful smile lighting up the day

Stop the kids that went out to play…

Her joyous screams, wild and free,

A gift so wondrous and joyful, given to me…

Her beautiful eyes holding the promises of life and love…

Filled with dreams from above…

Unwanted by her father, but accepted by the Lord…

He comforts the fatherless, a job for him that's not hard…

She has touched many lives as far as she could…

Including her mother's who knew that she would.

A Wonder and a Delight

Her big pretty brown eyes looking up at me…

as she asks what's wrong,

my tears she could see and through them,

I marvel at how much she's grown...

I thank God for giving her to me...

my blessing, thank you Lord for allowing this to be...

We've seen some good times and some bad,

but through it all I've still managed to be mommy and dad...

I want to protect her and I want her to have the best,

I don't want her to have anything less...

You enabled me to juggle her, college courses, and being a single mom,

I marvel at the big helper that she has become, I feel I've done a good job...

We've came a very long way and, I'm desiring better things for us,

I know that you will supply, in you do I trust...

Her laughter fills the air as she plays with her toys...

forever do I want, her life to be enjoyed...

She's my blessing and I don't regret bringing her into this world,

thank you Lord Jesus for blessing me with my little girl.

Note:* I know that there will be many people that will purchase this book just to read my personal testimony. The person that you are reading about is who I used to be long before I knew Christ, but not who I am now! My past doesn't dictate one thing about who I am now and I thank God for his many blessings because without his blessings, I wouldn't have been granted "favor" that no man can stop! I have made the Lord my habitation and there's nothing or noone that can take away from me who he has molded me to be...so this is just what it is: a testimony because we overcome by the blood of the lamb and the **WORDS OF OUR TESTIMONY**. We all have a past but some people are too ashamed to tell it or want to sweep it under the rug as though it never happend, but God sees all and he knows all, and there's nothing that we can hide from him. Then there are some such as myself that have a ministry of telling it so others can get free! Just as Prophetess Bynum Weeks told hers in No More Sheets, I tell mines, I'm not worried about what "people say..." because I'm not living for people, but I'm living for God so if you come to read this page, read it with an open mind.. Just like you are sitting or standing reading this, my parents (both) have read this and there is nothing that they do not know about me that I haven't told them already. ^-^*

Selah!
Make it a habit to become a blessing and not a condemer of others while you yet live. **LET THE MIND OF CHRIST BE IN YOU AT ALL TIME IF YOU SAY THAT YOU BELONG TO HIM!**

This book is a release for me for not only did I tell you about some of the things that I got caught up in, but I give you some solutions of how to get and remain free. It wasn't an easy battle because I tried in my own strength. When I learned that this battle was not mines but the Lord's, I found true deliverance and have to constantly ask Jesus to help me to maintain my deliverance. The minute you let your guard down by being spiritual lazy, the Devil is constantly looking for holes in your spiritual armor and when he finds one or some, he will squeeze his way through unless you patch up that armor, you will forever struggle with finding and maintaining deliverance. True freedom comes with knowing that you are free. You are not free just because you cry and scream at the altar, but you're free when you surrender your all to Jesus and say yes to God and surrender totally and mean it. Jesus knows our hearts better than we do and the unwillingness to confess sin because you are tired of battling will allow the same sins to keep resurfacing over and over again. Remember woman of God and woman of dignity and strength, this battle is not your's but it belongs to the Lord! If you purchase my book, (when it's available from revision), I pray that my testimony helps you and lead you to find true deliverance as I have in Jesus Christ. I call my book the Greatest Part of Me because truly Jesus is the reason why I live, move, and have my being. After going through so much in my life, I discovered the love of Christ like I never have before. I didn't give up even when I fell beneath his will, I didn't make excuses, but I got up to keep trying again. Although I still face many battles I will never cease in telling the world that Jesus truly is the Greatest Part of Me. I thank God for the many blessings that he has and will bestow upon me and my daughter's life. No one knows my story. There were times when I didn't know which way to turn. There were times where I felt like I would never amount to anything. I sought refuge in the wrong things and I didn't know how to come out, other than seeking God who pulled me out, but only because I wanted to come out! There are people that stay in bondages because they want to be there, but I wanted to come out of my situations never to look back at them again.

There are many people that judge people by their past, but they fail to realize what a person is and has become by the grace

of God. There are many religious people that sit back and watch you to see if you really are who you say that you are, but in

spite of the watchful eyes of those that's waiting for me to mess up or fall down, by watching me, make sure YOU don't be the

one to stumble. Daily I have to run this Christian race just as you do and if we say that we belong to God, then we should all be

striving for the same prize in Christ Jesus right? I'm striving to make heaven my home so in spite of if I'm up or if I happen to

stumble, there's only one man that's worthy of either looking down on me or picking me up and I thank God that he is not like man and he chooses to pick us up when we fall. Not only do he pick us up, but he places our feet on a solid rock to stand. It's truly a blessing to be here to declare his praises and to stand on his word, for truly I don't know what I would do without him!

I have been through an awful lot in my lifetime, but as each new day passes, I'm learning that I had to go through what I went

through in order to help someone else. At the age of 3, I almost drowned in a puddle of water. Me, my girl cousins and a family

friend's daughter were playing ring around the rosy. It had just rained and water was everywhere. At that time, Boyce had

poor drainage systems so the water would back up in the yard. We called ourselves playing on the porch pretending we were

going to push one another off into the puddle, we held hands swinging each others's arms back and forth really hard each of us

trying desperately to hold on for dear life so no one would fall in. It just so happened that the family friends daughter yanked me

so hard and I ended up falling in. I remember being in that water. You may ask me how do I remember that age age 3, but I'm

telling you, I remember it so clearly. The water was murky and I begin to cry. I heard the screams and I heard my grandmother and all them that were in the house came out screaming and fussing. The family friend's oldest daughter Theresa pulled me out.

My hair was really long reaching all the way down my back and I believe that she pulled me by my hair and that's how she got me out.

After that ordeal at age 4, I got ran over by a car where my parents thought I had died, but I survived that ordeal with only a bruise on my arm that still bears the mark of that fateful day.

At age sixteen, I lost my virginity. I listened to my friends that told me that sex was all this and that, but my first time was very

painful...not to mention the guilt that I felt because I lost my virginity to my boyfriend at the time and a few weeks later, we

went our seperate ways when I saw him walking down the hall embracing another girl that was supposed to be one of my so-

called friends at the time. From there, he and I dated on and off and eventually I got tired of being his doormat and I moved

on. I had a few boyfriends, but never had sex with all of them. Sex was spaced out in between..I would go for months without it,

but then I started going through so much in my family and my school work was beginning to become affected. After the death

of my grandfather, I went into a stage of shock and depression. I didn't want to talk to anyone, didn't want to come to school,

and I just felt like the whole world was against me. I turned once again to sex and this time, I became a little more active than I

had ever been. I was bleeding on the inside and just didn't know who to turn to. It wasn't to the point that I was giving myself

to every man that cames along, it was mostly with guys that were either my boyfriend or men that I was kicking it with at the time.

I couldn't tell my parents for fear that they wouldn't accept me, (I know now that was a horrible lie from the enemy), I couldn't even confide in my siblings. I would often get alone to myself and cry for hours at a time. I would always stay in my room and I kept my distance from everyone that could read into me. I begin to write, play my keyboard and sing often...that was the thing that got me through the rest of my teenage years.

When I became a young adult, things started to get a little better for me but I walked around with tremendous pain following me still. I didn't know anything about deliverance so therefore, I just carried my guilt with me everywhere I went. I was hooking up with drug dealers for boyfriends because I had that mentality that was as good as I could get...that's what I always attracked and that's what I got.

Me, my cousins, and a few of my cousin's siblings on their mother's side had a gun pulled on us one night. I was just an innocent bystander going with them to fight a girl from our school. That same night, I also confronted a girl that had been spreading lies about me. I was getting into behavior that I normally didn't harbor...but after that night, I no longer let my friends and cousins influence me to do anything because that girl's step daddy could have shot all of us that night. Bullets do not have anyone's name on it and it always be the innocent one that get killed!

I went back into my state of sullen silence after that incident. So much was happening to me at one time and it didn't seem like anything would go well for me.

By age 23, I was pregnant with my first child for my boyfriend at the time. I moved out of my parents house and moved in with

him. I had everything that a woman could probably hope for...he brought me things, he took me out, he spent time with me

whenever he felt like it. I stopped working to attend college and let him take care of me...the only thing that I didn't have was

him totally 100 percent. He would leave me at home alone with his then eight year old son to go out and party, drink, and run

women at the time I was naiive about the fact that he had other women besides me for if I would have known then, I

wouldn't have never put up with his mess. We barely got along. I knew I was pregnant and just didn't know how to go home

and face my parents. I was a wreck emotionally and I didn't know who to turn to. I would occassionally drink although I knew I was carrying my child, but I thank God that he took that habit away from me because there was another life besides me to

worry about and in spite of what her father was doing, I still had to go on and take care of myself and my unborn child. I had to be here for her in spite of if he wasn't doing his part. I can tell you woman of God about raising a child alone without the help of

the baby's father. It takes a real woman to do that and a real macho man to take care of his children especially his sons.

A son needs his father. It's sad that men can pass judgment on women who are raising their families alone, and trying to make

ends meet. You don't even know the half of how it feels to bring a baby in the world and then to take on the responbility of

caring for your family and bettering yourself because you want you and your child to have the best. That's why it's very

imperative for a woman to stop laying down with every man that comes along and laying up fornicating and committing

adultery period! Everybody mostly that knows me know that I do not play and I just tell it like it is...people can't stand it but I

can't sugarcoat it and stir sugar up in nobody's coffee...going through has made me tough; tough in the Lord and tough in life.

I've kept myself every since 2002 when I left Shania's daddy and I'm going to continue to keep myself pure, holy, and chaste

until my wedding night and I don't care what man don't like it or want me to bow down at their whim, I'm not going to

apologize that I don't fit your image because that's your image and I don't have to live up to it. I'm married to my Savior until I

marry. There will be no playing in this house because my body is the Lord's temple and I give myself wholly unto him.

During that awful season of my life, my baby's father would come home tore down drunk where he reeked of nothing but

alcohol and he would pass out on the couch. One night he called me out of the bed and he went and got his son out of his

room and came sat him on the couch. (his son is handicapped). He told me to sit down and he begin telling us both how much

he loved us and then he just fell out on the couch in his drunken state in midsentence. It was a very digusting sight to watch

and just to know that his son was watching him in this state. I couldn't believe that I stayed with him that long. I remember one

night having a horrible argument with him. Being pregnant, I was stressed, frustrated, and afraid, so in the middle of that

arguement, I fell on my knees and started praying out loud and crying out to God right in front of him.

Let me tell you a little secret women: I don't care what you try to do: If a man is not for you, he's not for you...let a man go

through a process of proving himself to you because there will be many pursuers but one special man that God has ordained

and chosen for you. So knowing that will keep you from alot of heartbreak and giving yourself to every man that comes along.

You can lose weight, get plastic surgery, ect...we can't go around or even try to change God's plan. You see I was making

plans for a wedding and thinking it was going to be one, but God came behind me and said otherwise and I still stand single

today, so don't think you can get bigger than God and make your will and desires become HIS! The church needs to hear this

because we have many pew riders thinking that God has to bow down at their every whim, but I beg to differ with you: "We

bow down to him and he doesn't bow down to us!"

After the doctor confirmed I was pregnant and when I caught him in the the very ACT of cheating on me when I came to our

home and found another woman (his so called best friend) in the bed that we shared, I moved out of his home that very night taking everything that I could and the things that I didn't, I left them there and I moved back in with my parents. I was so

heart-broken and stressed out, but I knew that it was harmful for me and my child and I decided why be stressed about s

omething that wasn't God's will anyway. Hmm...God's will and God's plan...we have a tendency this day and time to want our will to be God's will failing to realize that our lives are already pre-destined...what won't be it just won't be. If we would learn to

do God's will instead of our will, it would save us the heartbreak and the drama, but some people still choose travel down a

road of doing their will and yes, (a road of open disobedience and rebellion), God can use that experience to work his perfect will if a person is sincere enough to receive his taking over to lead and guide them!

I had severe morning sickness but by four months, I was doing pretty well. I didn't have anymore complications until I reached my eighth and ninth month. I had severe pre-eclampsia and had to be admitted to the hospital because my blood pressure (top number) was in the 200's and my bottom number was climbing behind my top number, but I never experienced any headaches, sickness or any of that and was only alive because of the grace of the Lord!

Because my blood pressure was not improving, they had to induce my labor a week early. They started me on the drip (Pitocin)

and I begin to experience contractions. I didn't have time to breathe in between any of them and they were coming back to

back. I was in so much pain that a nurse came in about five hours later and gave me Stadol...and the whole room started to

spin. I found myself drifting off into the unknown. All faces around me became blurry. My mom's, my sister, my doctors, ect...I

could hear their voices which was becoming muffled...I then noticed a team of doctors and nurses coming in...one had a EKG

machine. I was dying and I knew it....I started asking; "What's happening to me?" And my voice was beginning to sound far away. My mom said that my dad had just left the hospital and she called him back and told me to hurry up and come back because they were losing me. My dad said he called mostly everyone in the family and told them to begin to pray. My grandmother and my uncle had gotten really emotionally upset...and right now today those very two are deceased.

My dad came back to the hospital and he and my mom joined hands and begin to pray. My doctor stroked my hand and I

heard him say "Stay with us Ms. Peterson." His voice sounded very distant. I tried to keep awake for a voice was saying deep

within me, whatever you do, don't go to sleep. I was losing the fight because I felt so sleepy and I was drifting farther and farther into darkness. I knew my soul would have perished that night if I had died....but God in his splendor and his mercy kept

me here!!!!! I rejoice today because I'm here...I had a purpose and the Lord kept and preserved me through the most trying

time of my life! That was not my first near death experience, but it was the most scariest one because if I would have died that ngiht, I would have been hell bound because I didn't have God on my side, but I thank the Lord for giving me a chance to get

saved and delivered! This is not nearly half of my testimony and my book doesn't even tell it all but my new book "I'm Not Going

to Be Less than the Woman God Has Called Me to Be..." Will have more of my life story in its recent context.

I just truly thank God that I'm still pressing forward! It has been four years since that fateful day and I'm growing stronger and

stronger in my walk with God. Through all of my trials and tribulations, and my imperfections, I found Jesus and I'm no longer

that sullen teenager walking around feeling worthless and dejected...I found a place where I was accepted and that's in the

arms of Jesus. No matter who rejects me and don't like me for who I am, I know that Jesus loves me and his love for me will

never change. I thank him for embracing a sinner like me...taking me in the brink of my trials to a higher place and allowing me

to see my worth... I'm worthy because of him, but without him, I am worthy of death...but he looked death in the face and said,

"Not so!!!!" "She's mines and she belongs to me!"

Thank you Jesus!

To the broken woman that's reading this page that think that there is no way out, I want you to tell the Devil that he is a liar!

Jesus is the way out in fact, he is the only way out! A man can't heal you.

A man can't deliver you, and a man can't be God.

Our Father is calling us to come back to our first love! Some of us walk around broken looking for a man that is perfect and that can complete us. Even holy women in the church walk around broken still looking for a greater love when God has told her that

waited for the Samaritan Woman at the well, he's waiting on you to realize your worth that only he can bring out! A man can't do that for you! Many people love according to their flesh and what their eyes can see, but Jesus loves you according to your spirit....true love is loving me for my spirit, and not for what I look like. There's a difference between love and lust and lust is not love! Sadly, many people don't experience this type of love where the spirit is loved and nutured. We can't be loved from the flesh that love doesn't preserve!

Most women in the church are broken, they are trying to be single mothers of children, work two and three jobs, take care of a

family and run a household and they are looking for acceptance, peace of mind and they want to be healed! Not all women

come to church looking for a man...most women are coming to church to get free!

There are some women in church that's still in bondage and don't know how to let go of the pain that they are carrying. They

are still just wanting to be loved but they haven't realized that Jesus loves them and that there isn't one man that's fashioned

to love her more than he does. That empty space in your heart women of God can only be filled by him. I don't care how much

a man smiles at you, embrace you, kiss your lips and hold you at night, Jesus is still the void filler and if you know like I do if he

can't marry you after spending a considerable amount of time with you, then you don't need to waste your time with someone

that don't even know if he's going to make a committment to you. Know your worth!!!! And don't just marry the first thing that

comes along...let God give you your mate. Just because he attends church doesn't make him your Boaz! Use your spirit of discernment and allow God to dictate and order your steps. Don't get caught thinking that a man can save your emotions because he can't!

Stop stepping up on territory that's not even for you. You deserve what God has for you and if you're with someone that's

reserved for someone else, do yourself and him a favor and let God's will be done.

Trust me....take it from someone that knows...I've had an engagement broken a few years back and the excuse was that he

wasn't ready for marriage, but the truth that I drew from the situation was that he only wanted to go through an

engagement just to see if I would go back on my vow of not having sex until I married, how sad! He went through all that

trouble even asking my dad for my hand in marriage only to come a few months later and say that he wan't ready, but just like

he wasn't ready for marriage, I kept my vow and kept my clothes up. No wed no bed! No contract, no contact! Most men will only do what you allow him to do. Don't fall prey to the enemy's deception! I recommend Prophetess Bynum's book; "No More Sheets," to those that are recovering from sexual sins. It's a wonderful read and I know you will enjoy it.

The anointing on your life woman of God is very pricey and it cannot be put into the presence of just no any and everybody.

That's why God prepares a man that can handle your favor as a woman of God and he has to **RESPECT AND ACKNOWLEDGE**

you as the woman of God that you are. He is not to **MINIMIZE YOUR ANOINTING OR PLACE YOU IN A BOX BECAUSE THE**

ANOINTING CAN'T BE HID! God **IS** raising up women mouth pieces to proclaim his gospel and men are going to have to

understand that there is no respect of person in Christ. So whether a man or a woman preach, it's the Holy Ghost that's doing

the work! Once we die to flesh and stop teaching for doctrine the commandments of men, we would understand that and stop fighting about who is or isn't called to preach. Women of God, I want to encourage you to keep on striving for more of

God in spite of everything that you're facing right now. God loves you and he's not going to leave you to fend alone.

God wants you to realize your self worth and not depend on anybody else to be what he alone is to you in your life. I pray that

this helps you to understand that Jesus is waiting on you today to totally surrender and sell out to him. The choice is up to

you...for you don't have to keep worrying about who your husband will be, how you and your kids are going to make it or how

you're going to get out of what you're in...He has made the provisions, but he needs your trust. Will you come to him just as you

are?

Note to My Readers

I pray that you are blessed ten-fold by my testimony. I didn't know that I would be ministering in this book, but I just placed here what was upon my heart to be given to you. The enemy has silenced many individuals about their past and instead of them getting free from the pain inside it's eating away at them. I have held things in for so long, but I decided for myself that I wanted to be free. This book was not easy for me to write, but nevertheless, I feel so much better just by getting what was bottled inside of me on paper. Healing has begun in my life by the Lord allowing me to start my ministry and to minister freedom to those that are bound in the chains of the devil. After all of the hurt, the past sins, and the guilt, not only did I find deliverance, salvation, healing, and restoration, I found the greatest part of me and that's Jesus Christ. It was only through him that I found peace of mind, love, wisdom, guidance, strength and joy to overcome my past. I searched far and wide for a way to release this pain inside of me, but it was when I learned to come before God in my broken and contrite state that I found healing. It's indeed a divine blessing to be able to be used by God not only as an author, but as an evangelist, prophetess, psalmist, and most of all a mother to the daughter that he has blessed me with. Jesus means so much to me...I can never began to describe how much I love him. I hunger and I thirst for only him and now that I'm complete in him, I see things the way I have never saw them before. Right here and right now, I want to say: I forgive all those that have wronged me in the past I am no longer sullen and no longer do I hold a grudge against those who wronged me. In order to heal, we must learn to forgive. I'm not saying that we will ever forget our past...but I do believe one day that it will become a distant memory to those who want to heal, and move forward. I pray that you are blessed ten-fold by this book and I will close with a final word of encouragement for the entire body of Christ.

Much love,

Evangelist Shanetria Y. Peterson

A Vessel of Honor...Only Complete in Jesus Christ,

The Greatest Part of Me...

All of the hurt, all of the guilt, all of the feelings of worthiness that I felt at one time, it was Jesus that raised my head up, dried my eyes, and let me see through my blinded eyes just how important I was...I have heard many saints in the body of Christ shoot people down when they tell them that they are still dealing with some hurt from their past. INSTEAD of sending them away with an encouraging word, they tell them such things as: "Get over it!" or something else...they don't give them a word from the Bible that's going to encourage them. We need to learn how to minister encouragement to that person walking along who may feel that the weight of the world is on their shoulders. We never know what emotions are going through a person's mind and heart. That person could be suicidal and just one word of encouragement may get them to change their mind and turn their lives over to Jesus or hang on to their anchor if they already have a personal relationship with him.

Healing is a process that no one but God can take a person

through. No one can tell you how to heal and give you a time limit to heal...One thing for sure, God can heal all wounds if you continue to trust him and allow him to heal you. The first step in healing is admitting that you are hurting and that you need to be healed...

Become transparent before God, confess to him all hurt that you are feeling...and at that moment forgive all those who have wronged you. From one that has been hurt tremendously in the past, I can tell you to take your hurt to J-E-S-U-S and allow him to heal you. I can assure you that it's a process and it does not happen overnight, so the time table that man comes up with you can throw it out of the window! Mending may be a process, but it restores your heart and as time goes along, that hurt will become a distant memory.

> Then your light shall break forth like the dawn,
> and healing shall spring up quickly.
> Isaiah 58:8

My son, attend to my words; incline thine ear unto my

sayings.

Let them not depart from thine eyes; keep them in the midst of thine heart. For they are life unto those that find them and health to all their flesh.

Proverbs 4:20-22

What better person can we think of when we hear wounded and bruised
but Jesus?

But he was wounded for our transgressions he was bruised for our iniquities; the chastisement of our peace was upon him; and with his stripes we are healed.

Isaiah 53:5

After all Jesus went through on our behalf, he was raised up in complete victory.

After conquering the cruel beatings, the cross, the grave, and hell, Our Savior rose as a testimony to us...

When you are hurting go to God and ask him to heal you...man is not a problem solver...take your hurt to God in prayer for he is the only one that can heal and restore you. He can also direct you to wonderful sisters and brothers in Christ who will not discourage you, but will embrace you and pray you through whatever hurtful situation you are facing. As a Saint, we look for the encouragers and not those that always have a negative word such as: "Get over it!" or "You are supposed to be a Christian, don't feel that way!" I don't care how holy we think we are, we all get hurt and bruised along this journey....Jesus is the healer and the restorer...just because we are Saints does not mean we are super human beings incapable of being wounded.

Heal me, O Lord and I shall be healed; save me,
and I shall be saved; for thou art my praise.

Jeremiah 17:14

More healing from hurt scriptures

For I will restore health unto thee, and I will heal thee of thy wounds,

saith the Lord; because they called thee an Outcast, saying, this is Zion, whom no man seeketh after.

Jeremiah 30:17

For every one that asketh, receiveth; and he that seeketh,

findeth; and to him that knocketh, it shall be opened.

Matthew 8:8

Jesus Christ the same yesterday and today and for ever.

Hebrews 13:8

There was a woman the other **day**, sitting on a bench with tears streaming down her **face**...she was well known in the **church** ,but, she was clearly bruised and **hurt**.

Another woman came **by**, Recognized her and said **hi**...The woman looked up and wiped her **face** but, the hurt could not be **erased**...The woman walking by asked what was **wrong**...The woman told her story; it was painful and **long**...The lady walking by told her with disdain in her **voice**,

you are a Christian, you don't hurt; you **rejoice**. The lady that was crying told her, we hurt **too**, but, I have learned to depend on Jesus when I'm **bruised**...see we try to act as though we are super human,

that's a deception taught by the **church**, to appear macho before man...all of us get to a place where we **hurt**...

We shouldn't conceal that just because we're the **church**...but instead of letting bitterness set in our **hearts**...

We should take our hurt to Jesus so he can give us a new **start**.

Now It's Time for

Deliverance

Evangelist Shanetria Peterson

First and foremost, I want to thank my Lord and Savior Jesus Christ for without him, I would be lost. *I love you dear Father.~*

I would also like to thank my parents:
Reverend Earl Sr. and Evangelist Jacqueline Williams for being my mentors over the years.
Thank you both for teaching us the ways of righteousness.
I love you both with all of my heart.

I also want thank God for my angel:

Shania Ahmajay Peterson

IN
LOVING
MEMORY
OF
MY GRANDPARENTS
HERBET LEE WILLIAMS
ALICE MAE PETERSON
AND
JACK CLARENCE PETERSON

Table of Contents

Prelude pg. 4

Bondages pg. 6

Suppressed Sins pg. 11

The Pulling Down of Strongholds pg. 15

Eyes for Lust or Jesus? Mind for Pleasure or Jesus? Heart for Serving God or the World? pg. 21

Trials, Temptations, and Tests pg. 25

Mastery pg. 31

The Mess that We Make, But It Takes Jesus to Clean It Up pg. 37

The Heart is Deceitful Above all things and Desperately Wicked, Who Can Know It? pg. 44

My Personal Testimony pg. 50

Soul-Ties pg.55

Personal Note pg. 60

Prelude

It really and truly alarms and amazes me, the number of saints in the body of Christ that are saved, but have not been taught, "deliverance." Many of them are still struggling with sins of the flesh and accepting those sins as part of their character. What we need to know as being believers is that anything that's not pleasing to God is not healthy and we should not become comfortable with our sinful habits and tip them off as part of our character. Deliverance is so important! First let's define deliverance. Deliverance is to rescue from bondage or danger. You may look at this and say, "Well, I've accepted Jesus as my Lord and personal Savior, so I don't have to worry about being in bondage." Well, let's define bondage then in order to see our need for deliverance more clearly. Bondage is the state of one who is bound as a slave or serf. Okay, so now let's identify the slaves of our lives. It could be current enslavements or past enslavements. They could be smoking, gambling, drugs, bad attitude, lying, stealing, love of money, sexual sins, ect…only you can identify your slaves; those were just a list of examples. In coming to Christ and accepting him as our Lord and personal Savior, we went through the first process of receiving our deliverance. We may have prayed the salvation prayer and may have had a few scriptures recited to us and got baptized for the remissions of our sins and received the gift of the Holy Ghost. If this is the process that you have taken, well good for you but there's more! I was baptized first on April 20, 1985 at the age of five years. My parents weren't saved at the time so therefore, I didn't know the *meaning* of being baptized. One night during service at our old church, the invitation to discipleship was extended, and I remember it was a whole line of my peers that went up to be baptized including my sister and brother. (My youngest brother wasn't born at the time). We all went up to sit in the chairs to be baptized. Now over the years, I came to know that being baptized wasn't enough. I was still lying, still rebellious to my parents, ect... So people, let me clarify, the water baptism is just merely the first step. There is no magic in the water either! You have to see your need for deliverance and your need for Jesus Christ in your lives. You must also have to be sorry for the sins that you have committed and believe that Jesus is the true son of God, born of the Virgin Mary, (word made flesh) and that he lived a sinless life, died on the cross for our sins, and rose again on the third day with all power both heaven and earth in his hands over Satan. You must also know and see your need for deliverance which is an ONGOING PROCESS FOR EACH ONE OF US IN THE BODY OF CHIRST! You will see later as you read farther. Baptism is the water purification that symbolizes the cleansing (remission) of sins. Jesus said, "Most assuredly, I say to you, unless one is born of water and the Spirit, he cannot enter the kingdom of God" (John 3:5). At seven months pregnant with my first and only child, I was called into the ministry. Okay, I couldn't go and be baptized with a big stomach, so I told me dad who is also my Pastor that I wanted to be baptized (again) after I had my baby. (I never mentioned the call into ministry), so on March 29th 2005; I was re-baptized in the name of Jesus for the remission of my sins. My life has changed drastically since then, but I still did not see my need for deliverance! This is the reason for this book, for when I learned there was more, I sought out to find the missing link to the puzzle. If you have this book in your hand, I do not believe it was by mistake that it's there for in order for us to walk in the freedom that Jesus has given to us; we must be free from the bondages of our past sins, walk in our freedom daily and know that we are free! I pray that you are blessed by this book and read carefully from beginning to end.

Chapter One
BONDAGES

If you are still struggling with the flesh, then you are not alone! There are millions of Christians worldwide that are struggling with past sins that they have never been delivered from. Most of these Christians have not even been taught on the subject of deliverance. This is very important Christians, for we are living in the last and evil days and it's no time for us to be ignorant of this very important subject! In order for us to be free from sins, we must recognize our need for Jesus Christ daily and not just on Sunday's or at baptism time. It's sad that many of us as Christians walk through this life defeated without depending and relying on Jesus Christ to help us through our trials, tribulations, and struggles. Romans 8:37 reads: Nay, in all these things, we are more than conquerors through him that loved us. Are you a conqueror or do you cower at the first sign of trouble? Do you have any strongholds in your life? What do you do when you are faced with a trial that overwhelms you? If you are struggling with past sins, past hurts, setbacks, disappointments, the list goes on…then what are you doing to endure these things? Do you constantly find yourself fantasizing over past lovers? Do you constantly talk about the past? Are you still suffering from hurts endured during your childhood? Have you not forgiven yourself for mistakes that you have made over the years in your life? Amen. If you answered yes to any of these questions asked, then you need to allow God to heal you and free you from the bondages from the past. This is not a game of scrabble! Strongholds are indeed real and so is your need for deliverance! We do not snap our fingers and declare ourselves free! Only God can declare us righteous and not we ourselves! Many people in the body of Christ are walking around with their hearts on their sleeves still weighted down and heavy laden with sins and struggles. They are praising God, praying for others, and giving a word to encourage others, but deep inside they are angry, struggling with sin, bruised and bitter from their past sins and what people have done to them over the years. They have not practiced forgiveness, so therefore they do not see their need for forgiving the ones that have hurt them and their deliverance from those past hurts and sins . Let's talk about being free for a second or two. What do you think about the word freedom? Freedom is liberty of the person from slavery, detention, or oppression. Freedom is not constantly talking about past hurts, or still dipping and dabbing in sins of the past, that includes even looking back at those things that have happened in the past, or being oppressed and depressed over ones circumstances. There are many saints declaring that they are free, but they absolutely do not believe in their hearts that they are really and truly free from their bondages! What's even more alarming is that they are not walking in their freedom. Some are deceived into thinking that they are free when they haven't even been given the right to sing the freedom song! Freedom starts with 'KNOWING' that you are no longer bound in chains of the devil! The devil's purpose is to try and keep us in bondage. He once had a place in heaven: Let's see what happened that his place was no longer found in heaven. Revelation 12:7-9: "And there was war in heaven: Michael and his angels fought against the dragon; and the dragon fought and his angels, and prevailed not; neither was their place found any more in heaven. And the great dragon was cast out, that old serpent, called the Devil, and Satan, which deceiveth the whole world: he was cast out into the earth, and his angels were cast out with him". So he knows how heaven was for he was once there. Now since his place was no longer found there, he wants to make sure that you will not go there either! He wants to keep the body of Christ oppressed, burdened, and down-trodden. He wants to whisper in your ear that you will never be free from bondage, but you are going to have to reach a place in your life where you tell that old serpent to get behind you! James 4:7 says; Resist the devil and he will flee from you. Resist means to remain firm against the actions, effects, or force of; withstand:

You will have to reach a place in your life where you will believe that you are free from bondage. There are so many in the body of Christ that has bound the symptoms of their problem, but not the root. Okay, come with me prophetically for a second. We all know how irritating weeds are that may spring up in our yard unexpectedly or in our flowerbeds. Suppose you get a shovel and chop down the top portion of the weeds but you never get the source of the problem and that's the root. What you have done was get rid of the symptoms which was the weeds, but you did not get rid of the root of that weed where they were able to grow, so what's going to happen? It will spring up again! This is the same way in bondages. You can go around and bind the symptoms of that particular bondage, but not ask God to get rid of the root. That's why many saints find themselves in a backslidden state and why many go back and grab the alcohol bottle, or the cigarettes again, because they have not been delivered from the root of the problem. They must confess to Jesus that they are an alcoholic or a heavy cigarette smoker and admit that they need help, see their need for help and allow God to start the deliverance process in their lives. God is the only one that can grant person deliverance. It isn't granted by good works or by good conduct. 1 John 1:9 reads; If we confess our sins, he is faithful and just to forgive us our sins, and to cleanse us from all unrighteousness. You must come to the knowledge of the truth that will keep you free. Just mere confession of your sins with your mouth isn't enough! You must be sincere in your heart. You must come to the knowledge of the truth that you need God's help throughout your walk and growth with him! Do not rely on your own strength for you will fail every single time! Deliverance **starts with** confession with your mouth with a sincere heart that you are in need of deliverance. You must also come to the knowledge of the truth that will keep you free. Don't let the enemy keep whispering to you that you cannot be free! John 8:36 reads; He who the Son sets free are free indeed." Do not expect your freedom to come all at once just because someone else told you that they were free from their bondages instantly, most deliverance processes is step by step and it is ongoing! We grow in grace and in the knowledge of our Lord and Savior Jesus Christ. Just like the Israelites took their land little by little, city by city, and battle, by battle, we must take everything the devil stole from us little by little. Exodus 23:29-30 reads; "I will not drive them out from before thee in one year; lest the land become desolate and the beast of the field multiply against thee. By little and little I will drive them out from before thee, until thou be increased, and inherit the land." We can only fight one battle at a time. We must keep on fighting until we possess and inherit our land. Many of us in the body expect our healing and deliverance to come at once. This is not poof magic done with a wand that magicians use. Deliverance is a process! Many of us want God to answer our prayer requests right then and there. We want to go through this life getting quick healings, deliverance, ect... We must learn the word patience, and we will be taught the definition of the word patience on this journey. We also must learn how to humble ourselves in the presence of the Lord. It's too many boasters in the body of Christ sticking their chest out trying to take the credit for God's work in them! Remember saints, your blessings may be delayed, but not denied according to God's will for your life! Just by you giving your life to Christ is the first step. Coming to Christ doesn't mean that your seat is reserved or that you have gotten a ticket to go to heaven, we must walk with the Lord daily and come initially to him in salvation. Bondages are servitude to Satan; you do not have any control over your inner struggles when you are undelivered. That's Satan's ground to hold over your head. That's his tape to stick you to a bulletin board any time he sees fit to do so. This is not what God wants for us. He sent his only begotten Son that whosoever believeth on him should not perish but have everlasting life. God doesn't hold any of us in bondage! He wants to see us free, but most importantly of all, he wants us to see our need to be free and rely on him to keep us free. We do not serve Jesus by compulsion. What is compulsion? Compulsion is an irresistible impulse to act, regardless of the rationality of the motivation. We do not serve Jesus out of compulsion. We serve him because we want to do so! God does not want us to remain in servitude and sin when coming to him. We cannot serve two masters, either we love one and hate the other! While God is cleaning and sanctifying us bit by bit , Satan is working trying to take back lost ground by deception. Many Saints do not have enough word or no word at all to know the tactics of the devil. Satan transforms himself to an angel of light. When you do not know your word, you don't have anything to fight him with so therefore, He can use that stronghold to bring you into a greater bondage than you were at first! We don't get into bondages of the devil all at once. Bit by bit, we listen to one lie of the devil who has set up a snare for us to break one of God's law, and when we break that law, he will whisper another lie into our ear to leave us to make the decision of breaking another one of God's law. Know he sets the trap, we fall in and it snaps shut! He does not pull any of us by our arms to make us fall for his tactics. Deeper and deeper, you go into the grasp of Satan when you keep listening to his lies and deceptions. If you do not have any firm ground of God's word to stand on that's the devil poison to feed you! That's why the church is so much in an uproar. There are ministers that are not teaching deliverance because either they are not delivered themselves, out for personal gain, deceptive, stubborn, do not care for their flock, or either they are just plain ignorant on the subject. They are ministering the word of God to most in the body that are undelivered vessels who do not have any ground in their heart to receive what's being ministered to them. They are still dipping and dabbing in sin thinking that it's okay for them to still sing in the choir after clubbing all night long or serve on the deacon board with a wife on the front bench and a mistress sitting on the deaconess board. Why is this happening? It's simple: they are accepting the notion that it's okay for them to behave in this manner because of the deceitfulness of their own hearts. Satan has deceived the church for so long until it is beginning to look like the world, but take heed to this message! It's time to stop being deceived by the devil! The Church needs to be delivered! Ecclesiastes 10:8 says; He that diggeth a pit shall fall into it; and whoso breaketh a hedge, a serpent shall bite him." Many saints are adding sin on top of sin progressively. Just like sin is added progressively, so is our deliverance. We must allow God to remove those areas that Satan has access to bit by bit in order to move on to complete victory in Jesus Christ! The cause of all bondage is sin! All unrighteousness is sin! John 5:17(a) says; "All unrighteousness is sin." 1 John 3:4 says; "Whosoever committeth sin transgresseth also the law: for sin is the transgression of the law." Romans 14:23 (b) says; "for whatsoever *is* not of faith is sin." James 4:17 says; "Therefore [conclusion] to him that knoweth to do good, and doeth *it* not, to him it is sin." There are many in the body of Christ who want to twist the scriptures around for their own selfish benefit and it's deceiving them into thinking they are doing what's right when they are walking in total disobedience to God's word! There are many that do not want to be told that they can't fornicate or commit adultery and still be holy, or that they can't lie and still be called holy, or that they must pay tithes for the word says so, ect... We are the pollutants and not God's law! The word is right all by itself no matter how many people take it out of context, the word will still be the word! The church thinks that they can get away with sin because of the deceitfulness of their own hearts. Jeremiah 17:9 says; "The heart *is* deceitful above all *things,* and desperately wicked: who can know it?" Many think that they are walking in the way of God by sin, listening to the devil saying, "It's okay to gamble, long as you don't make it a habit." Or "It's okay to lie on your income tax, for it will get you more money." That's the problem with the world today, they think they are getting by with sin when actually, God is keeping a record of it all! He sees all and he knows all! Proverbs 14:12 reads; There is a way which seemeth right unto a man, but the end thereof are the ways of death. I had a man that I was ministering to this year to tell me: *"You can't tell me that having sexual desires for a woman is wrong."* He was deceived by his old carnal heart. For the old heart cannot understand the things of the spirit. Ecclesiastes 10:2 reads: "A wise man's heart *is* at his right hand; but a fool's heart at his left." A wise man's heart will direct him toward the right, to that which is right and a foolish man's heart will direct him to the left, to that which is wrong. When you hear people say, they are following their hearts, they may mean exactly that, for it will either lead them to the right or the left. We are not sinners because we sin, but we sin because we are sinners. We are born into sin! We do not have to teach our children to do that which is wrong for we were born into the sinful nature of our old carnal hearts! We must train them up to do that which is right! Proverbs 22:6 reads; "Train up a child in the way he should go: and when he is old, he will not depart from it." Proverbs 22:15 "Foolishness *is* bound in the heart of a child; *but* the rod of correction shall drive it far from him." Proverbs 29:15 "The rod and reproof give wisdom: but a child left *to himself* bringeth his mother to shame." It does not mention here that they will not stray away from it, for even if they do stray away from it, we as parents should not hold our heads down for they have been taught but they are the ones that strayed away from it! Keep reading for the new birth process and the renewal of the mind which is coming in later chapters. Reader, I really want you to see your need for deliverances. For the root of your past sins is the devil's stronghold to keep slamming you against the walls and keeping you in bondage. I pray this book will help you realize our need for deliverance. I can't free you, and you cannot free yourself, but by Jesus Christ, you will be free and only by him will you walk in your freedom!

Chapter Two
Suppressed Sins

So many people in the body of Christ have suppressed or un-confessed sins that's causing the same sins to keep resurfacing over and over again. What is suppression? Suppressed is o keep from being revealed, published, or circulated. How many Christians are putting on a smile and professing Jesus in public but behind closed doors, they are raising sand, cursing, lying, and committing shameful acts? If you are one of these people today, you may fool the public, but you are not fooling God! He knows all and he sees all! Healing and delivering cannot occur if we do not confess our sins! Unwillingness to confess sins will hinder the healing process. We can also hinder our healing process with the unwillingness to forgive others who may have wronged us in our lives. Mark 11:25-26 "And when you stand praying, if you hold anything against anyone, forgive him, so that your Father in heaven may forgive you your sins." I have heard Christians say with their mouths that they can forgive people who may wronged them but they can't forget! Their unwillingness to forgive others will be the devil's stronghold for him to constantly keep grabbing that root so when they see that person, hear that person's name or think about what that person done to wrong them, they will allow the devil to bring anger and bitterness in their hearts against that person. If we cannot forgive and forget the sins of others, then we are not walking in the example of Christ. We need to understand the power of forgiveness! If you do not realize your need for deliverance and how important confession of your sins are, you will never see clearly until you heart is purified by the blood of Jesus. The problem with most of today's churches is they are playing church instead of really and truly having church. They go in do a little worship, preach a sermon that doesn't move anyone to repentance, and many in the body leave out the same way that they came. Some people believe just reading their bibles, listening to the preacher, and coming the church is all there is to live "saved." There is a life that we have to live! We have to live a life of sanctification. When many people come to Christ, they do not confess their sins in complete sincerity or confess them at all. They say, "Lord forgive me of my sins." They do not confess the roots of their past sins. They also do that out of what they feel is a duty to them receiving salvation, but it's not in their hearts. Preachers that preach the once saved always saved sermons really and truly make me cringe! Church members are getting deceived when they receive that notion! The Apostle Paul notes in Acts 3:19-20 reads; Repent ye therefore, and be converted, that your sins may be blotted out, when the times of refreshing shall come from the presence of the Lord. And he shall send Jesus Christ, which before was preached unto you. There are many in the body of Christ that do not simply want to give up all of their sins. They feel in their hearts that fleshly pleasure and desires is too good for them to give up so they walk around professing Jesus with their mouths, but their hearts are far from him. "These people draw near to Me with their mouth, and honor Me with their lips, but their heart is far from Me. And in vain do they worship Me, teaching as doctrines the commandments of men." {Matthew 15:8,9} Many people are trying to lead others to Christ with their old religious traditions and the nature of their sinful hearts. How can a farmer receive milk from a cow if he doesn't know how to milk her? How can he receive the milk if he doesn't have anything to put it in? Reader, hear me today! It's imperative that the church realize their need for deliverance, for many people are being deceived by their old sinful hearts and nature. Is that sin so important to you that you can't let it go? How can you serve God out of a heart full of sin? Do you trust that Jesus has paid the price for your sins? Do you believe that Jesus can deliver you from your past bondages? We have got to stop being religious, stubborn and close-minded to where God is trying to take us. If we do not receive help for ourselves, sin is going to eventually destroy us and cause us to be cast into outer darkness! Why do sins keep resurfacing? Because many saints are trying to serve God out of their old carnal hearts and have not asked God for the new heart transplant. We will get more into that in a later chapter, but I want you to understand that old hearts and un-renewed minds can deceive souls into thinking that they are in good standing with God when in actuality he doesn't even know who they are! Many religions and organizations are being deceived about demons and demonic oppression. Many circles believe that Christians cannot be oppressed! This notion is based on an assumption and has not been backed up by scripture! Who do you think the devil is after of? Is it the person that he already has or the now Christian that he have lost! Come on church use your sense of judgment! The devil is not going to run after people he already have! His job is to charge after the Christian to try to turn them back to sin! He is trying to win back ground that he has lost! One reason why we have so many Christians with suppressed sins, is because they are either too ashamed to admit it's there or they are accepting those old habits as a part of their character. The church is ever learning but never coming to the knowledge of the truth and this is indeed scary in this last hour! The Apostle Paul tells us in 1Thessalonians 5:23 that man is a tripartite being: spirit, soul, and body. God has created a three-fold salvation. (Created in the image of his threefold creator). When a person is born again, he is burst with new energy and the new life and presence of God. [Justification] serves to liberate the person from bondages in the soul. Regeneration in the spirit does not mean that person has received complete salvation and has moved on to perfection. The second-fold includes the daily process of cleansing, changing, conforming, and renewing the soul into God's likeness. The soul is composed up of a man's mind, will, and emotion which are indeed not perfect! This is where bondages [the root of bondages] and sins of the past are found. The soul is slowly transformed to become a pleasing habitation of the Lord. This process is called sanctification (or set apart unto holiness.) Finally the third part of our salvation involves our body. When Christ comes back again, scriptures tell us that we will be changed and shall receive new bodies like unto the Lord's new body after resurrection. This is called glorification. In justification (our past salvation) we were delivered from the penalties of our sins. [external salvation] In sanctification (our present salvation), we are being delivered from the power of sin in our lives each day. In glorification (our future salvation), we shall be delivered from the presence of sin altogether!

SCRIPTURES THAT INDICATE CHRISTIANS CAN HAVE DEMONS OR BE OPPRESSED

(Please Study this!)

- Matthew 15:22-28 Deliverance is the 'children's bread;' and is therefore particularly reserved for believers
- Matthew 16:22-23 Jesus rebuked the spirit of Satan speaking through Peter
- Mark 1:23 A man with an unclean spirit 'in the synagogue'
- Mark 1:39 Jesus cast out demons 'in the synagogues'
- Luke 9:52-56 Jesus told James and John, '...you know not what spirit you are of'
- Luke 13:11-16 A 'daughter of Abraham' was bound by a 'spirit of infirmity'
- Acts 5:3 Satan 'filled the hearts' of two believers to lie to the Holy Spirit
- Acts 8:13, 20-24 Simon, a believer, needed deliverance from the occult
- 1 Cor 5:1-5 Speaks of a believer filled with a spirit of lust and as a result, delivered over to Satan
- 2 Cor 2:10-11 Satan can 'get advantage' over a believer
- 2 Corinthians 11:4 Paul rebukes believers for receiving 'another spirit'
- 2 Corinthians 12:7 Paul was tormented by a 'messenger from Satan'
- Galatians 3:1 Paul rebukes believers for being 'bewitched'
- 1 Timothy 1:19-20 Speaks of two believers who were delivered over to Satan for blasphemy
- 2 Timothy 2:24-26 Believers can be snared and taken captive by the devil
- 1 Timothy 4:1-2 In latter days believers will give heed to seducing spirits and doctrines of demons
- Ephesians 4:25-27 Lying and anger can 'give place' to the devil in a believer's life

Many Christians are being deceived into thinking that

once they are saved, they are always saved so therefore they do not receive freedom from their bondages. That's how people are snared into cults and other demonic activities for lack of discerning and knowing the word of God. Many organizations are walking around in spiritual pride with a holier-than-thou attitude and believe that their salvation is secure, but they are still holding on to past sins and traditions that's causing them to walk in total disobedience to God's word! Habitual sin will cause the Holy Ghost to depart from that individual because he cannot dwell in an unclean temple.

Holier-than-thou attitudes are grounds for the devil to come in and snatch that Christian and whip him or her everywhere. He hears your prideful boasting and he will come and test you to see if you are really rooted and grounded in that area as you boasted to others that you are free in. Pride is a bondage that requires deliverance too! See my friends, when you hide or suppress your sins, that's another way saying that you are not ready to give up that bondage. If you harbor this attitude, you will not become free! Church, you need to know that we have a short time to get our houses in order and it comes with us being real with ourselves! We need deliverance!

Chapter Three
The Pulling Down of Strong Holds

What is a stronghold? An area dominated or occupied by a special group or distinguished by a special quality: Whether you want to accept this notion or not, Satan is real! And he wants to dominate and control your life. His demonic forces are also real and they are running rampant with him deceiving many. There is power in the blood of Jesus Christ! You have to know the weapons of our warfare and use them! 1 Peter 5:8 reads; be sober, be vigilant; because your adversary the devil, as a roaring lion, walketh about, seeking whom he may devour: We must know of the ways that we can be caught off guard!

When we stop reading our word, when we stop fasting, attending church, and stop being in the presence of the Lord, those are some ways that we can be caught off guard! Many of us in the body of Christ find ourselves in despair when we are going through trials and tribulations. This is a fairly easy way for Satan to come in and prey on our weakness. If there are holes in our spiritual armor, this is ground for Satan to get through and gain access to lost ground. He wants you to be in despair about lack of finances, your job, and your family situation, ect...for that's a way for him to get in and try to mess with your mind to distract you from God. Satan knows our weaknesses and if we are not delivered, he knows how to keep springing the root of that undelivered problem to surface. The world is constantly tormented with desires, falsehoods, lying, maliciousness, hatred, disobedience; ect...our natural affection is to fight back with whatever weapons are available. Satan is ready to arm our emotions with weapons that may seem needed during our dark trying times and our periods of despair. He preys on our weaknesses being the thief that he is! It's extremely important for the body of Christ to learn spiritual warfare prayers and to rely on Jesus Christ who is the problem solver for all situations! Do not get me wrong saints, we all go through our trying times and we have many things that slaps us in the face all at once, but that's when we should look up and know that Jesus is there to help us, even when we fall! We must know that Jesus is a present help in a time of the storm and he doesn't expect us to wallow out in self pity but to get back up, confessing our sins, ask him to forgive us and keep fighting! Staying down gives the devil room to move in and play patty-cake with your mind and heart. Do not give him place in your life! Satan wants us to fight our warfare in the flesh. His tactics are used to try and deceive us into thinking there's a better way to handle our problems instead of turning to Jesus, but you must know that the devil does not have any power or authority over Jesus Christ and the ground that he has won from that sly serpent! Trust in the Lord today with all that you have and believe that you can be free, don't doubt him, but walk in the victory that Jesus has won for you! Be strong in the Lord and the power of his might! Our brother Paul has given us some instructions and list our weapons in Ephesians 6:14-18 Stand therefore, having your loins girt about with truth, and having on the breastplate of righteousness; And your feet shod with the preparation of the gospel of peace; Above all, taking the shield of faith, wherewith ye shall be able to quench all the fiery darts of the wicked. And take the helmet of salvation, and the sword of the Spirit, which is the word of God: Praying always with all prayer and supplication in the Spirit, and watching thereunto with all perseverance and supplication for all saints;

- **Truth**- The foundation of our armor. The truth is all in the word of God. It's important for us to speak the truth of God's word, obey the truth of God's word, accept the truth of God's word, and live the truth.

- **Breast Plate of Righteousness**- Guards our heart against the devil's attacks. To be declared righteous, we must follow God's commands. When we dwell on our own righteousness, presumptions, theories, and even when we speak truth to others and don't believe in it ourselves, we are doing this independently aside from God. We weaken our positions when we follow our own logics and ways instead of that of God. This is a firm ground for the devil to set up pride which is one of the seven things that God hates! 16:5 reads; Every one that is proud in heart is an abomination to the LORD: though hand join in hand, he shall not be unpunished. Proverbs 16:18 reads; Pride goeth before destruction, and an haughty spirit before a fall. Do not follow after your own theories. Turn back to the Lord! Our ways are not like his ways and our thoughts are not like his thoughts.

- **The Gospel**- Our foundation and stability to walk in the righteous place of life. We must walk in the truth no matter what! We must not compromise the truth or sugarcoat it! We must remain firm in our stand on God's word. Romans 1:16 reads; For I am not ashamed of the gospel of Christ: for it is the power of God unto salvation to every one that believeth; to the Jew first, and also to the Greek.
- **Shield of Faith**- Our shield to defend us against attacks from all attacks. If we exercise faith in our lives, powerful things can happen to us just by believing and stepping out on our faith! Don't be caught without it! There are many in the body of Christ talking faith, but in their examination of the fruit of the spirit, they do not have it! This is the most important ingredient to our walks with God, our FAITH TO BELIEVE IN HIM and BELIEVE WHAT HE CAN AND WILL DO IN OUR LIVES! WITHOUT FAITH IT'S IMPOSSIBLE TO PLEASE HIM!
- **Salvation**- This is our helmet of hope and trust. (Head protection), knowledge, appreciation and understanding of God's word, divine plan and purpose of our lives. (Our divine destiny).
- **The Sword of the Spirit**- The Holy Bible is the only offensive weapon of the Christian. It is sharper than any Two-Edge-Sword. Hebrews 4:12 reads; For the word of God is quick, and powerful, and sharper than any two-edged sword, piercing even to the dividing asunder of soul and spirit, and of the joints and marrow, and is a discerner of the thoughts and intents of the

heart. We must study our word carefully and ask God for divine revelation of what's written in his word.

We do not fight our battles like the world fight. We fight with the word of God! Daily we should look up to God for strength, comfort, and protection. If we depend on our own strength, we will constantly fall miserably! God is able to do anything but fail! He can fail if he wanted to, but he chooses not too! We fail, but God does not! 2 Corinthians 10:3-5 reads; For though we walk in the flesh, we do not war after the flesh :(For the weapons of our warfare are not carnal, but mighty through God to the pulling down of strong holds ;) Casting down imaginations, and every high thing that exalteth itself against the knowledge of God, and bringing into captivity every thought to the obedience of Christ. How are you pulling down your strongholds? If you do not know how, let me give you an example of an effective weapon. Prayer! Have a specific prayer that you pray for the particular temptation you are faced with. Every time the devil comes against you with that particular temptation, be armed and ready with that prayer. God answers sincere prayers! Satan will not come at you in that particular area when he knows that particular area will be met with an immediate offensive attack back on him and his kingdom. We have to learn to trust God in our deepest hour of temptation. He will never leave us nor forsake us. Here's an entry I wrote on my media journal back on June 15, 2006 to encourage the body of Christ that God is no short of his word:
Praise the Lord Saints of God. It's indeed a divine blessing to be found in the presence of God once more and again. It's another day's journey and I am glad about it. I don't care what trials, tribulations, setbacks, and disappointments may have littered your table today, God is still the same today, yesterday, and forever and he is going to work out your situation for you!
Praise the Lord, people change constantly, situations change constantly, our government words, our president words, and other people's word may change constantly, but it's a joy and a wonder to know that God and his word never changes.
Seasons change, situations and circumstances change. Amen. Think of all the things that change, but God never change! His word will never

change: if he promised us a blessing according to his will for our lives, he doesn't change his mind about it; it may be DELAYED, but not DENIED! We must get in the proper order if we're not already, and if we are in the proper order, it's imperative to stay there! Push prayer and praise until something happens. Don't give up the fight, don't throw in the towel, if he said that he would do it; it will come to past. I'm encouraging someone today as well as myself, somebody out there may be hanging on by a thread, but I come to tell you today, to get ready for your blessing is on the way! Don't get distracted or caught up in worrying about when it's going to happen, or what your situation may look now, for you just might miss it! Fall in and line up with God's word, God is not a man that he should lie! It bothers me when people say that God said this, and God did this, then turn around and say, well, maybe he didn't want me to have this blessing, or no, God didn't speak this after all, if he spoke something into existence for you, then it is so, he will not come back and change his mind about what he spoke to you! God cannot and will not lie, he can do anything, but fail, he could if he wanted to for he's God, but he chooses not to! He won't say one thing and then come back and say something else. That's not how God operates. So when we say that "God did or said something, we must make sure that God said it and did it," For if it's him, everything will fall into place for you!" Hold on and keep the faith!
We're living at a time now where we got to make sure we are doing and speaking God's will over people's lives. It's important for us not to be playing with God's word.... (Oh speak Holy Ghost,) We as Ministers will be held accountable if we're speaking things contrary to God's word, ouch Holy Spirit, it may hurt us but keep on speaking.....We got to make sure we are heeding to God's instructions, his doings, and his voice and not our own. We can't live off of presumptions and assumptions, we can't tell God's people to live off of presumptions and assumptions, make sure it's God that's speaking before you speak into someone else's or over someone else's lives. A true sheep know his Shepherd's voice. What God does, it SHALL BE DONE.
Thy kingdom come, thy will be done in earth as it is in heaven...that's his word, it won't return to him void, for it's written...speak to God's people what is written, don't beat around the bush, don't butter it up, speak the word for it's written, and it won't change, it won't be one thing one day and something else tomorrow. The Constitution may change, hallelujah, the sun may shine one minute and storm clouds may raise the next, but God and his word, WILL NEVER CHANGE. Don't be a Covenant Breaker, don't be someone who live off of presumptions and assumptions, for if you operate in this mode, God can take his anointing off of you. Seek the Lord, incline your ear to his voice, and make sure it's God's word. And when others speak something over or don't judge or condemn it but, check it with the word of God. ALL THINGS SPOKEN TO US SHOULD LINE UP WITH

GOD'S WORD. The word is our instruction manual, for every subject that you need an answer to, it's in there!
This stanza was spoken into my spirit the other night, "Make Sure it's God...."
Amen, I don't know who this is for, and it's not for me to find out.....in all that you do in your life, "make sure that God is laying and has laid your foundation. God never changes his mind people and neither does his word change.
No scriptures is here today, just giving you straight what God has given me to say to you. Whoever this is for, receive God's word in faith, hope, and love and remember, it may be delayed, BUT IT'S SURELY NOT DENIED. God's word never change and neither does he.
May God have a blessing upon the reader, but most of all the doer of his Holy Word~Yours, In Christ..

God never changes no matter what we may be going through. He has given us the weapons to fight to good fight. It's time for us to cast down imaginations and every high thing that lift itself against the knowledge of God. We see so much of his happening in our world today. Theologians, our governments, our president, ect...they try to figure out God and measure their knowledge against his knowledge! They try to use earthly logics and reasoning against spiritual reasoning. Our ways and thoughts are not that of God so we cannot began to understand his ways. Our imaginations are very powerful and they can be used for good or for evil. When we use our imaginations for evil, we let our minds fill with the evil thoughts that Satan puts there. For instance: pornography. Just one image can create a motion picture in ones minds of that particular image...lust sets in along with idolatry of that person or the act itself and those imaginations are raised up against God. We have the weapons to cast them down! We must not allow the devil to cloud our judgment in using those weapons and using them effectively! God has provided the way for us to escape. Praying in the spirit can help shift our thoughts to God and to tap into the Holy Spirit to overcome that temptation! We must learn how to guard our minds against the devil's attack, for if we do not stop measuring our knowledge against that of God and if we do not bring into captivity every thought to the obedience of Christ, the devil is going to keep us in bondage and dominate us until we make a stand in Jesus Christ that we are going to fight for our deliverance and walk in our deliverance for the rest of our lives! He's not going to flee with our tears our shouting at him to leave us alone! We must use our weapons given by God mightily and believe in our hearts that they are going to defeat him!

Chapter Four
Eyes for Lust or Jesus? Mind for Pleasure or Jesus? Heart for Serving God or the World?

It bothers me when I see saved single women or man lusting after a men or women.
 If we are supposed to be examples to the world, then how can we lead if we can't come up under the subjection of the Holy Ghost? How can we give advice to others about sexual sins and holding out until marriage if our own flesh isn't crucified? Sexual lust with the eyes is a very serious factor, and it's just as dangerous as committing the very act!
Mathew 6:22 NKJV reads; "The lamp of the body is the eye. If therefore your eye is good, your whole body will be full of light." Long looks can lead to lust. That forceful craving for personal pleasure or gain is intensified by the fix of our focus upon the object of our desire. Eve stared at the forbidden fruit, wondering on its possible potential. David stared longingly out his window upon naked Bathsheba bathing. Samson perceives the beauty of Delilah more desirable than the strength of God. Think about this: Just at the moment that God may want to use you to pray for someone or to go out and minister, your mind could be snapped out of focus by the enemy causing you to be distracted from God's purpose, and instead of God's divine purpose, your mind is then bombarded with thoughts of a man (women) or a woman, (men) that's not your husband or wife, or some other desire that will keep you from remaining focused on

what he is asking you to do for HIM. An unfocused mind can lead to destructive behavior and it can also reap consequences in our walk with God. Ever heard the statement, "Just one look that's all it took?"
Amen....ponder on this statement and read about David's lust just by looking and then acting on those desires:
Bathsheba lived near the palace.
(2 Samuel 11:2) "And it came to pass in an evening tide, that David arose from off his bed, and walked upon the roof of the king's house: and from the roof he saw a woman washing herself; and the woman was very beautiful to look upon." David could see her from the roof of his palace, and he saw that she was a beautiful woman.
Bathsheba was wed to a man of power and integrity.

Uriah was a captain in David's army. He is listed in the twenty-third chapter of the book of second Samuel as one of David's thirty mightiest men. (2 Samuel 23:8.39) "These are the names of the mighty men whom David had: Uriah the Hittite: thirty and seven in all."
After David received the word that Bathsheba was pregnant with his child, he tried to lure Uriah from the battle into the arms of Bathsheba in the hopes that Uriah would believe the child was his. Uriah was a very dedicated and honorable man and wouldn't take any pleasure or interest, even in his own wife, until the battle was won.
A woman is aroused by the touch of a man but a man is "turned on" just by the sight of a woman. (It takes a match to light a fire), if she is a beautiful naked woman, a man will be turned on at the first sight of her. Bathsheba was not just pretty but, David saw her nakedness. That's all it took for him to get aroused. He lusted in his heart and with his eyes. (James 1:14) "But every man is tempted, when he is drawn away of his own lust, and enticed."
David lusted. That was one of his first sin. **(Matthew 5:27-28)** "Ye have heard that it was said by them of old time, Thou shalt not commit adultery: But I say unto you, That whosoever looketh on

a woman to lust after her hath committed adultery with her already in his heart." He was desired and was about to act on those evil desires in the flesh.

This chapter is not to tell the entire story of David and Bathsheba, but to sum it all up:

David sinned when he lusted after another man's wife and he had sex with a married woman. David was aware of the penalty for adultery was death for he knew the law. That's how easy it is to go into a sexual bondage, just by looking and lusting!

Our eyes are the windows to our souls. What we allow through that window can affect our choices. Jesus clarify this principle when He declares:

Mathew 5:28 NKJV: "But I say to you that whoever looks at a woman to lust for her has already committed adultery with her in his heart.

The devil knows how to entice us. He knows our weak points and things that will cause us to become distracted. If that factor is lusting after a man (ladies) or a woman, (men) He'll dress that temptation up and if you're not careful, he will cause you to lust after that person. Look at the above verse, "But, I say to you that whosoever looks at a woman to lust for her has already committed adultery with her in his heart."

Just a look could cause sin, just an "ooh wee, he is fine, I got to get with him!" (ladies), or "ooh wee, she is fine, I got to get with her!" (men)

Do you realize that Jesus is more important than a momentary stare and sexual desire of a man or a woman? Do you realize that your soul is more important than desiring something or someone that is off limits to you?

The look that leads to lust is not one that happens by chance through a quick glance. It is premeditated and fixated. It perceives, regards, and takes heed, giving full vent to fantasy and imagination. As we continue to allow our minds to enjoy the visual video through the windows into our soul, we fuel the desires of temptation that give birth to sin. And that sin leads us into bondage! Temptation comes from the lure of our own evil desires and it's not that the devil made us. These evil desires lead to evil actions, and evil actions lead to death. (James 1:14-15)

The connection between your visual intake and your thoughts that lead to choices is so strong (the devil knows this) billboard signs, t.v. commercials, and Internet advertising use it for a foundation. Internet website creators use it, and Marketers know that what looks good will sell and entice the mind. Why? Because it creates an image, which produces a thought to form in your mind, which gives birth to a desire, which dictates a decision. This scenario caused David to conclude that the only way to stay pure is to guard the gate of his soul: If lusting after a woman (men) or a man (women) is your weakness, confess your sin and ask God to deliver you from this area.
 if sexual lust of a man or woman is not dealt with, un-healthy soul ties and bondages cause trouble in your walk and causes the same sin (lust) to resurface over and over again if not dealt with.
Just by looking at a person with your eyes and desiring them sexually can cause you to become SOUL-TIED to that person and you must be delivered to be set free from that bondage!~ JUST ONE LOOK AT A PERSON TO DESIRE THEM CAN CAUSE TROUBLE. Some people in the body of Christ is still walking tied to others and haven't asked to be delivered from that person. They have committed adultery in their hearts just by looking and imagining sex with that man or woman that's not their spouse, and they must ask God to free them from that tie. This is very serious! Soul-ties will be mentioned later.

Mat. 5:29,30: "And if thy right eye offend thee, pluck it out, and cast it from thee; for it is profitable for thee that one of thy members should perish, and not that thy whole body should be cast into hell. And if thy right hand offend thee, cut it off, and cast it from thee: for it is profitable for thee that one of thy members should perish, and not that thy whole body should be

cast into hell."
it doesn't even have to be the physical act! Lust (PERIOD) is a distraction from Christ it could be behind material things, amen, things of the world, ect....keep your mind focused on Jesus and do not let the devil distract you!

Study

James 4:1 - What causes fights and quarrels among you? Don't they come from your desires that battle within you?

James 4:2 - You want something but don't get it. You kill and covet, but you cannot have what you want. You quarrel and fight. You do not have, because you do not ask God.

James 4:3 - When you ask, you do not receive, because you ask with wrong motives, that you may spend what you get on your pleasures.

James 4:4 - You adulterous people, don't you know that friendship with the world is hatred towards God? Anyone who chooses to be a friend of the world becomes an enemy of God.

James 1:13 - When tempted, no-one should say, "God is tempting me." For God cannot be tempted by evil, nor does he tempt anyone.

Matthew 5:27 - "You have heard that it was said, 'Do not commit adultery.'"

Matthew 5:28 - But I tell you that anyone who looks at a woman lustfully has already committed adultery with her in his heart.

Proverbs 6:25 - Do not lust in your heart after her beauty or let her captivate you with her eyes.

1 Peter 2:11 - Dear friends, I urge you, as aliens and strangers in the world, to abstain from sinful desires, which war against your soul.

Titus 3:3 - At one time we too were foolish, disobedient, deceived and enslaved by all kinds of passions and pleasures. We lived in malice and envy, being hated and hating one another.

Titus 3:4 - But when the kindness and love of God our Savior appeared
Titus 3:5 - He saved us, not because of righteous things we had done, but because of his mercy. He saved us through the washing of rebirth and revival by the Holy Spirit. Do not let lust bind you!

Chapter Five
Trails, Temptations, and Tests

Praise the Lord Saints of God!!! I don't know about you, but I feel like praising the Lord on this glorious day that the Lord has made! Many of you may be wondering about this vessel, but I want to inform you! God is still in control here and will always be no matter what I have to face what trials and test that I may have to endure, the way have already been paved and made and I'm going to walk worthy according to the will of God.
Psalms 37:1 Fret not thyself because of evildoers, neither be thou envious against the workers of iniquity.
2For they shall soon be cut down like the grass, and wither as the green herb.
 3Trust in the LORD, and do good; so shalt thou dwell in the land, and verily thou shalt be fed.
4Delight thyself also in the LORD: and he shall give thee the desires of thine heart.
 5Commit thy way unto the LORD; trust also in him; and he shall bring it to pass.

6And he shall bring forth thy righteousness as the light, and thy judgment as the noonday.
7Rest in the LORD, and wait patiently for him: fret not thyself because of him who prospereth in his way, because of the man who bringeth wicked devices to pass.
Last week was a week of testing for me and the tests is not over with. People of God let me tell you this today: get ready for you will be tried! You will be persecuted, tested, and tempted of the devil on every hand, but God has given us power to overcome. We're no different than Jesus was when he was tempted of the devil, but just like he overcame, we can too if we learn to use the word of God against our situations, (storms, tests, trials,) It's what we will do when we are tested that's going to prove out how strong we really are in the Lord, and how suited up we are in our protective armor. I want to talk about the word tempt for a brief second.
Definition of tempt
1. To seek to attract and persuade someone to do something, especially something wrong or foolish.
Thesaurus: entice, lure, bait, tantalize, seduce, coax, enamor, woo, incite, draw, allure; Antonym: discourage, dissuade.
2. To attract or allure.
3. To be strongly inclined to do something.
Form: be tempted to
4. To risk provoking, especially by doing something foolhardy.
Example: tempt fate
Just because we are strong in the Lord does not mean that we will NOT be tempted! The devil will use whomever or whatever he can to try and divert our attention away from God and our purposes in him. Examples: He can use another saint, an ex-lover, financial situations, and children, ect…to try and tempt you. See he knows the area of your life that used to be your weak points before you were converted, and this is no time to try and avoid the situation!!! It's time for us to learn to stand our ground and defeat the devil out of our lives with the word of God! And when we overcome, remember, he will come again with something else!!!!! But, we have been given the authority

to use against him and his Angels! Will you use your God given authority? There's no time to be comfortable and idle, for the battle in this spiritual warfare is constant...when we overcome one thing, LOOK OUT!! There's going to be something else that will come along, but we have been given the AUTHORITY!!!!
Fight fair,
Fight hard!!!
Your Battle is already won
In the Lord!
Don't try to run and go the other way,
Stand your ground and fight the devil
For the way of defeat have already been paved!
Luke 10:19 reads: Behold, I give unto you power to tread on serpents and scorpions, and over all the power of the enemy: and nothing shall by any means hurt you.
Romans 12:21Be not overcome of evil, but overcome evil with good.
1 Corinthians 10:13 There hath no temptation taken you but such as is common to man: but God is faithful, who will not suffer you to be tempted above that ye are able; but will with the temptation also make a way to escape, that ye may be able to bear it.
Word of Encouragement for the Body

I press toward the mark for the prize of the high calling of God in Christ Jesus~Philippians 3:14

Praise the Lord who isn't just the head of my life, but he is my life. I thank the Lord for letting me and my family see a brand new day. I thank God for each and every last one of you, and I pray the blessings of God rain upon your life. I thank God for the rain and for the sunshine on this glorious day of his. Praise the Lord Oh ye people of God, and make a joyful noise unto our only Lord and Savior and that's Jesus the Christ.
Today, I want to talk about moving forward.....
How many of you know that yesterday is gone and tomorrow may never be ours to behold? Amen, everything that

happened on yesterday, whether it was good or bad, I can't go back and change the bad things or neither can I dwell on it. The past is the past. When we sincerely give our life to Christ, that means surrendering everything over to him. Many of us, (especially women), like to dwell on the past...but we can't live our life in the past. Whatever happened in the past is over with, and in coming to Christ, the slate is wiped clean. Are we preventing our slates from being wiped clean totally? Are we still harboring ill feelings toward someone that wronged us 5-10 years ago? Are we still dwelling on past hurts that have wounded us? Amen...God is doing a new thing in the lives of the Saints, and it doesn't involve those places that WE have been, amen, it involves our place in him right now, and the place that he wants to take us if only we allow.

Isaiah 42:9
Behold, the former things have come to pass,
Now I declare **new** things;
Before they spring forth I proclaim them to you.
Isaiah 43:18, 19
Do not call to mind the former things,
Or ponder things of the past.
Behold, I will do something **new**,
Now it will spring forth;
Will you not be aware of it?
I will even make a roadway in the wilderness,
Rivers in the desert.
Isaiah 48:6-8
I proclaim to you **new** things from this time,
Even hidden things which you have not known.
They are created **now** and not long ago;
And before today you have not heard them,
So that you will not say, `Behold, I knew them.'
You have not heard, you have not known.
Oh I praise you Lord Jesus for doing a new thing in my life. I thank you Lord Jesus for wiping the slate clean so I can start afresh, for without that fresh start and that new manna, I

wouldn't be able to survive if I keep looking over my shoulder at the things that have happened yesterday. Glory to God. We can't dwell on yesterday's promises and yesterday's anointing, today is a new day and we are to declare a fresh anointing in our lives for that fresh anointing is needed for whatever I have to face on today. Yesterday's experience is not going to be the same as today's experience so I need a fresh anointing for each day I live.

New Anointing, New Joy, New Hope, but the same Vision to see the Lord

"But my horn shall thou exalt like the horn of the Unicorn, I shall be anointed with fresh oil" Ps. 92:10
"And the yoke shall be destroyed because of the Anointing" Isa. 10:27
"The Spirit bade me go, nothing doubting" Acts 11:12
"Whereupon I was not disobedient to the heavenly vision" Acts 26:19

Your anointing is your anointing, and no one else can lay claim to your anointing. There is a story behind your anointing, there's a reason why you praise God the way that you do. There's a reason why you are still here today, because if the devil would have had his way with you; you would have been dead a long time ago, but oh by God's grace, mercy, and fresh anointing in your life, YOU ARE STILL HERE! God is doing a new thing, fulfilling new promises, restoring things in your life; not the way that it was at first, but a NEW THING. There's no need to expect the old thing. If you keep on looking at the old, you will never receive the new!

Keeping Our Eyes on the Prize

In order to keep our eyes on Jesus, we got to keep looking forward, how can we see him if we're looking backward? How can we see him if we are still dwelling on yesterday's events? Keep your eyes focused on Jesus, our prize....we ought to reach a point in our life where we can boldly stand up and proclaim, no distractions, no hindrances, no past hurts, ect...can keep our eyes off of the prize! Philippians 3:13 reads, 13Brethren, I count not myself to have apprehended: but this one thing I do, forgetting those things which are behind, and reaching forth unto those things which are before. KJV

None of us have it made, but we should be well on our way, reaching out for Christ who have reached out for us. I don't have time to look at your walk, I don't have time to see who is coming behind me, I can't dwell on what's behind me, I can't keep looking over my shoulder to see if you're with me, I got to keep pressing....no matter what trials and tribulations come....I got to keep pressing, no matter what snares the devil throw for me to get tangled in....I got to keep pressing, because I'm a joint-heir with Christ and I'm fighting daily to keep my inheritance, I got to keep pressing because I'm determined to keep fighting. Keep marching saints of God...keep hoping, keep believing....I refuse to judge and look down on you, I rather reach out my hand to grab you and we can keep striving for the prize together on one accord, aiming for the same mission and that's to see Christ's face. I'm not a Bible scholar, I don't know everything there is to know that's written in the word of God, and I don't dot every i and cross t. I have faults, I have shortcomings, I find myself confessing and repenting of sins every single day. I'm not inferior to you, I'm a servant just as you are....I'm your sister in Christ, and I have your back just as I expect you to have mines. I got my eye on the prize and I'm striving, will you go with me? I got my eyes focused forward and I'm not looking back. I'm pressing my way, through hot stinging tears streaming from my eyes, trials, tribulations, setbacks, heartaches and some pain. You don't know my story and can't tell it like I can. I don't know your story and I can't tell it like you can. Don't desire to be like me, but desire to be like Jesus who knew no sin and error. Don't desire my anointing, for you don't know what I had to go through in order to get my anointing, it's a price that you have to pay; it's a cost that you have to count up. Will you count up the cost for your anointing? If you're already counting up the cost or have counted it up already, will you keep striving? When they persecute you and call you everything but a child of God, will you keep holding on? Will you continue working in the vineyard? Will you learn to love your enemies and bless the ones that curse you? It's a heavy price to pay to strive for that prize, but if you keep your eyes on it; you won't go wrong.

I won't say that you won't fail, for daily, we're falling short of God's glory, but will {you/I ~talking to me} get back up confessing your {/my~talking to me} faults to God and keep striving?

Forget those things behind you today Saints, and keep moving....
Allow God to break those Un-Godly Soul-Ties, Bondages, Generational Curses, ect....so you can keep striving for the prize. Don't let the devil lead you astray to a road that leads to destruction, but stay on the road where Jesus is taking you.....no matter what you have to lose in order to gain Christ.
 Philippians 1:21For to me to live is Christ, and to die is gain.
 22But if I live in the flesh, this is the fruit of my labor: yet what I shall choose I wot not.
 23For I am in a strait betwixt two, having a desire to depart, and to be with Christ; which is far better:
24Nevertheless to abide in the flesh is more needful for you.
 25And having this confidence, I know that I shall abide and continue with you all for your furtherance and joy of faith;
26That your rejoicing may be more abundant in Jesus Christ for me by my coming to you again.
27Only let your conversation be as it becometh the gospel of Christ: that whether I come and see you, or else be absent, I may hear of your affairs, that ye stand fast in one spirit, with one mind striving together for the faith of the gospel;
28And in nothing terrified by your adversaries: which is to them an evident token of perdition, but to you of salvation, and that of God?
 29For unto you it is given in the behalf of Christ, not only to believe on him, but also to suffer for his sake;

30Having the same conflict which ye saw in me and now hear to be in me.
Philippians 3:1If there be therefore any consolation in Christ, if any comfort of love, if any fellowship of the Spirit, if any bowels and mercies,
2Fulfil ye my joy, that ye be likeminded, having the same love, being of one accord, of one mind.
3Let nothing be done through strife or vainglory; but in lowliness of mind let each esteem other better than themselves.
4Look not every man on his own things, but every man also on the things of others.
5Let this mind be in you, which was also in Christ Jesus:
6Who, being in the form of God, thought it not robbery to be equal with God:
7But made himself of no reputation, and took upon him the form of a servant, and was made in the likeness of men:
8And being found in fashion as a man, he humbled himself, and became obedient unto death, even the death of the cross.
9Wherefore God also hath highly exalted him, and given him a name which is above every name:
10 That at the name of Jesus every knee should bow, of things in heaven, and things in earth, and things under the earth;
11And that every tongue should confess that Jesus Christ is Lord, to the glory of God the Father.

Chapter Six
Mastery

Giving honor to God who is not just the head of my life, but HE IS my life. IN HIM ONLY do I move, live, and have my being. This week, we have been discussing the Power of Obedience from Prophetess Weeks book, "My Spiritual

Inheritance," today; I want to talk about a very important topic that can very well go along with this subject, for its highly important for us as being leaders:

How many of you have mastered something in your lifetime? Whether it was obtaining a High School Diploma, completing job training courses for your job, obtaining a college degree, ect...let's define mastery briefly: **(2.)** The status of master or ruler; control.

Amen, so in other words, it's to complete, to get complete victory over, to control an area, ect...so where could we use the word mastery in our walks with the Lord?

Let's look in the word for an example of where we as SAINTS may need to get our mastery certificate:

Romans 14:1 reads:
HIM that is weak in the faith receive ye, but not to doubtful disputations [the act of disputing, debate].

The word weak in this passage means "without power" or "little power

Verse 2 says: For one believeth that he may eat all things: another, who is weak, eateth herbs.

(This is just one example of this verse :) We have various groups of saved people that believe "he can eat all things"~ for instance, one may believe that he can accept God's word as is and not question what's written. He understands God's word; he's able to accept the strong meat of the word, ect...

We may have another group of saved people that are weak (eateth herbs), so in other words, he may be the one that question what's written or only receive a portion of it. (He weighs the pros and the cons of it), Then you have the group that hear the word and will not accept it at all. ~

So I used this example to say this, there are so many different degrees of strength among the body of Christ. Just because I may be able to digest meat, I cannot expect someone that's weak in the faith to be able to digest meat along with me, we're on two different levels and God is the only one that can bring him or her to spiritual maturity. Just because you can eat strong meat, consider your sister or brother who may not be

able to digest strong meat as of yet. So you must be careful with them, do you catch that in the spirit?
There are so many in the body that are trying to make others that are coming up in Christ jump ahead of their growth chart and get to maturity, but Jesus is the only one who is able to bring a person up to the level where he will have them to be. Skipping levels will cause them to miss something that's important in their growth. Amen, think of a newborn baby. You can't bring him or her straight from the hospital and start feeding them table food, what do you think will happen? It will cause them to get sick! Amen, we are to receive the weak in faith, this means we are to welcome them. We are to have special interest in them. We are not to remind them of their weakness or to condemn them, but we are to accept them as brothers and sisters in Christ, and make them feel welcome. We are not to engage in heated arguments about our differences. That's what the Bible is for, that's what preaching is for, to convict, correct, and rebuke.
Verse #3 reads: Let not him that eateth despise him that eateth not; and let not him which eateth not judge him that eateth: for God hath received him.
Verse #4 reads: Who art thou that judgest another mans' servant? to his own master he standeth or falleth. Yea, he shall be holden up: for God is able to make him stand.
Why do any despise? Why break off into arguments? When God himself hath received both parties? Do we have any right to count people out? If there are any corrections that need to be made, God can and will handle it without help from anyone. He does not need any help especially from us! That's what God have ordained word carriers and the Bible for ect... and that's for to convict, correct, and rebuke us to correct those things that need to be corrected in our walks, and to bring edification to us as a body. The word is not used to destroy each other and beat up one another with! ~
He that is weak and may not be able to digest strong meat today, but God is able to bring him to maturity so he will be able to digest strong meat on his set timing!

Verse #5 says: One man esteemeth one day above another: another esteemeth every day alike. Let every man be fully persuaded in his own mind.

Just because you may set aside each day of your life to glorify God without missing a beat, another may set aside another day to glorify God and have some space in between. We can't tell others what day or time to worship God, or what days that we should set aside to worship God, ect...so whatever day, hour, time, place, ect.... we decide to worship God, let every man be persuaded in his own mind, let the Holy Ghost convict him or her so they will follow the convictions of their conscience and not that of man.

verse #6 says:

He that regardeth the day, regardeth it unto the Lord; and he that regardeth not the day, to the Lord he doth not regard it. He that eateth, eateth to the Lord for he giveth God thanks; and he that eateth not, to the Lord he eateth not, and giveth God thanks.

Verse #7 reads: For none of us liveth to himself and no man dieth to himself.

Verse #8 reads: For whether we live, we live unto the Lord; and whether we die, we die unto the Lord: whether we live therefore, or die, we are the Lord's.

Verse #9 For to this end Christ both died, and rose, and revived, that he might be Lord both of the dead and the living.

So if you keep a holy day, keep it for God's sake, if you eat meat, eat it to the glory of God and thank him for it. If you are a vegetarian, eat vegetables to the glory of God and thank him for it. None of us are permitted to insist on our own way in these matters. Its God we are answerable to—all the way from life to death and everything in between—not each other. That's why Jesus lived and died and then lived again: so that he could be our Master across the entire range of life and death, and free us from the petty tyrannies of each other.

(Romans 8:1) There is therefore now no condemnation to them who walk not after the flesh, but after the Spirit.)

 Christ died for each and every last one of us. He died for the just and the unjust alike, so there's no need for us to answer to one another, to point fingers at each other, and try to put others on our spiritual level. God does the changing, God does the exalting, and not we ourselves.

Verse 10-12

But why dost thou judge, (reduce to nothing), why dost thou set at naught thy brother? for we shall all stand before the judgment seat of Christ. For it is written, AS I LIVE, SAITH THE LORD, EVERY KNEE SHALL BOW TO ME, AND EVERY TONGUE SHALL CONFESS TO GOD. SO THEN EVERY ONE OF US SHALL GIVE ACCOUNT OF HIMSELF TO GOD.

What does it profit to judge a brother or sister? Where does it leave you when you condescend to a sister? Eventually, we're all going to end up kneeling side by side in the place of judgment, facing God, so judging one another, pointing the finger at each other, is not going to matter for we all will end up at the judgment seat of Christ. If we're busy caught up dipping in others business then how are we watching our own walks? It's a battle just to keep self straight. We are wasting time beating up each other, when we should be out there winning souls to Christ and being about Our Father's business.

13-14 reads: Let us not therefore judge one another anymore: but judge this rather, that no man put a stumbling block or an occasion to fall in his brother's way.

So that means, when we tell others about the word of God, we should make sure we are practicing what we preach, we shouldn't behave in a way, present ourselves in a way that will not cause our brothers to stumble. Not everyone have achieved mastery of the flesh, not everyone eateth strong meath, so with the different levels in Christ, we shouldn't set up stumbling blocks to fall in others way. So if we say that we are saved, we should watch how we dress, our walks, our talks, ect....and be careful that we're not the cause of another man stumbling. We should be convinced that Jesus convinced us that everything in itself is holy. We by the way we can treat God's word, because we can contaminate it! So if we're going to bring someone else to Christ, we need to walk the walk, and

talk the talk and practice what we preach, watch how we present ourselves, ect....
for Romans 12:1-2 reads; IBESEECH you therefore brethren, by the mercies of God, that ye present your bodies a living sacrifice, holy, acceptable unto God, which is your reasonable service. And be not conformed to this world: but be ye transformed by the renewing of your mind that ye may prove what is that good, and acceptable, and perfect will of God.
15-16 verse reads: But if thy brother be grieved with thy meat. now walkest thou not charitably. Destroy not them with thy meat, for whom Christ died. Let not then your good be evil spoken of.
Do not be grieved, and do not confuse others by making a big issue over what they eat and don't eat. If you do that, you are no longer a companion with them in love. Christ died for the sinners. Don't let handling God's word deceitfully become an occasional stumbling block for others. Do not let others speak evil of your words, (for you may think you have good intentions by condemning them); but your "thinking good intentions by condemning them can be evil spoken of by the ones you condemn. Don't let it happen!
Verse: 17-19
For the kingdom of God is not meat and drink; but righteousness and peace, and joy, in the Holy Ghost. 18) For he that in these things serveth Christ is acceptable to God, and approved of men.
God's kingdom isn't a matter of what you put in your stomach. It's what God does with your life as he sets it right, puts it together, and completes it with joy. Your task is to single-mindedly serve Christ. Do that and you'll kill two birds with one stone: pleasing the God above you and proving your worth to the people around you. Come on, we can do it!
19-21
Let us therefore follow after the things which make for peace, and things wherewith one may edify another. 20) For meat destroy not the work of God. All things indeed are pure; but it is evil for that man who eateth with offence. 21) It is good neither

to eat flesh, nor to drink wine, nor any thing whereby thy brother stumbleth, or is offended, or is made weak.
So let's agree to use all our energy in getting along with each other. Help others with encouraging words; don't drag them down by finding fault. You're certainly not going to permit an argument over what is served or not served at supper to wreck God's work. All food is good, but it can turn bad if you use it badly, if you use it to trip others up and send them sprawling. When you sit down to a meal, your primary concern should not be to feed your own face but to share the life of Jesus. So be sensitive and courteous to the others who are eating. Don't eat or say or do things that might interfere with the free exchange of love.
Verse 22-23
Hast thou faith? have it to thyself before God. Happy is he that condemneth not himself in that thing which he alloweth. 23) And he that doubteth is damned if he eat, because he eateth not of faith: for whatsoever is not of faith is sin.
We should cultivate our own relationship with God, but don't impose it on others. You're fortunate if your behavior and your belief are coherent. But if you're not sure, if you notice that you are acting in ways inconsistent with what you believe—some days trying to impose your opinions on others, other days just trying to please them—then you know that you're out not in line with God. If the way you live isn't consistent with what you believe, then it's wrong.
The title of this chapter is called **"Mastery,"** and I used Romans 14 to make a point, that the strong and the weak should grow together. If we have Mastery over areas of our life such as the flesh ect...then it's our job to help someone else that may not have obtained mastery over the flesh yet. We do not have the right to judge or condemn them, but to help one another out. For Mastery also comes with us having the "mind of Christ," "Treating others the way that Christ did when he walked the earth." We didn't see him condemn others, nor did we see him uphold others in their wrongness, but he did forgive them and had compassion on them, so let us do the same!

God is looking for **Mature Masterers** that's able to help others and not use their mastery to trip others up or look down on the ones that haven't mastered their walk yet.
May God have a blessing upon the readers, but most of all the doers of his holy word.

Chapter Seven
The Mess That We Make, But it Takes Jesus to Clean It Up

This chapter may seem a bit strange, but if you are able to walk into the spirit, then come with me for a few minutes as I allow the Holy Ghost to bring this out according to the way he wants it to go, for if you are in the flesh, it's hard to understand what the spirit is saying to you. So do not check me in the flesh, but check me in the spirit, because the flesh will not allow you to see things in the spirit. It just doesn't work.
Just allow the Lord to guide your spirit, as his word penetrate inside of your mind, heart, and soul, so you can receive it and it can fall on good ground.
It will not return to the Lord void.
How many of you hate to make a mess? I know I do with a passion. There's truly something about a spill on the floor or a table that makes me cringe. The first thing that we do is run to go get something to clean it up, Amen. I really and truly hate a spill of red juice in a light colored carpet or on a light colored couch, because we know that dark ugly red spot, no matter how we clean and clean, it will take so much effort to get that stain out. Well, in my entry today, I'm not talking about a physical stain that we as humans make when we spill food, juice, or whatever item, but I'm talking about when we make a mess with our lives....Amen, every last one of us has made a mess of ourselves at some point or time, and some of us, instead of allowing Jesus to clean that mess up, we rely on our own strength, and then when our strength fail, the first thing we say is......
"Lord how am I going to get myself out of this?" Sounds familiar? A few examples of mess makers in the Bible, (This is just to name

a few)
Eve saw that the fruit of the tree of knowledge of good and evil was good and pleasant, and ate of it. {Genesis 3:6}
Cain killed Abel {Genesis 4:8}
The great flood that destroyed the earth. {Genesis 6:17}
Sodom and Gomorrah Destroyed {Genesis 19:25}
The Story of Samson (whose name means "sunshine") is one of great potential wasted through lack of discipline. Like King Saul, Samson had great potential, but squandered it. His enormous potential was wasted. Samson had: God fearing parents; a unique birth; unique lifestyle; great personal strength, and he was anointed by the Holy Spirit as a deliverer. But Samson became a weak man because he never learned to control himself. {You can read about Samson fighting with the Philistines in the 16 chapter of Judges.}
What we must learn:
"He who rules his spirit is better than he who captures a city." Proverbs 16:32
"Do not love the world nor the things of the world." John 2:15
"Friendship with the world is enmity toward God." James 4:4
Guarding our Spirit
The Holy Ghost is our instructor on how we are supposed to live as becoming saved and born again; we must be careful what we put into our spirit. We must watch what kind of spiritual food we feed our spirit, what can happen when a diabetic eat food containing alot of salt? Answer: Their feet may become swollen, ect...It is very important for diabetics to lower salt-sodium chloride-intake, as all too often diabetes is complicated by high blood pressure, a major cause of both heart disease and stroke. Many food manufacturers are recognizing the public's growing concern about salt and have begun to offer "reduced salt" or "no salt" alternatives. Restaurant owners are also more willing to prepare food with less salt-especially when asked to do so.
Amen. The same way a diabetic must take precautions with their salt intake, is the same way we must guard our spirit.
What is harmful to our spirit? You may ask me, Sister Minister,

how do I guard my spirit? Let's go to the word:

Romans 8

1There is therefore now no condemnation to them which are in Christ Jesus, who walk not after the flesh, but after the Spirit.
2For the law of the Spirit of life in Christ Jesus hath made me free from the law of sin and death.
 3For what the law could not do, in that it was weak through the flesh, God sending his own Son in the likeness of sinful flesh, and for sin, condemned sin in the flesh:
4That the righteousness of the law might be fulfilled in us, who walk not after the flesh, but after the Spirit.
5For they that are after the flesh do mind the things of the flesh; but they that are after the Spirit the things of the Spirit.
6For to be carnally minded is death; but to be spiritually minded is life and peace.
7Because the carnal mind is enmity against God: for it is not subject to the law of God, neither indeed can be.
8So then they that are in the flesh cannot please God.
9But ye are not in the flesh, but in the Spirit, if so be that the Spirit of God dwell in you. Now if any man have not the Spirit of Christ, he is none of his.
10And if Christ be in you, the body is dead because of sin; but the Spirit is life because of righteousness.
 11But if the Spirit of him that raised up Jesus from the dead dwell in you, he that raised up Christ from the dead shall also quicken your mortal bodies by his Spirit that dwelleth in you.
12Therefore, brethren, we are debtors, not to the flesh, to live after the flesh.
13For if ye live after the flesh, ye shall die: but if ye through the Spirit do mortify the deeds of the body, ye shall live.
 14For as many as are led by the Spirit of God, they are the sons of God.
15For ye have not received the spirit of bondage again to fear; but ye have received the Spirit of adoption, whereby we cry, Abba, Father.
 16The Spirit itself beareth witness with our spirit, that we are the

children of God:

17 And if children, then heirs; heirs of God, and joint-heirs with Christ; if so be that we suffer with him, that we may be also glorified together.

18 For I reckon that the sufferings of this present time are not worthy to be compared with the glory which shall be revealed in us.

19 For the earnest expectation of the creature waiteth for the manifestation of the sons of God.

20 For the creature was made subject to vanity, not willingly, but by reason of him who hath subjected the same in hope,

21 Because the creature itself also shall be delivered from the bondage of corruption into the glorious liberty of the children of God.

22 For we know that the whole creation groaneth and travaileth in pain together until now.

23 And not only they, but ourselves also, which have the firstfruits of the Spirit, even we ourselves groan within ourselves, waiting for the adoption, to wit, the redemption of our body.

24 For we are saved by hope: but hope that is seen is not hope: for what a man seeth, why doth he yet hope for?

25 But if we hope for that we see not, then do we with patience wait for it.

26 Likewise the Spirit also helpeth our infirmities: for we know not what we should pray for as we ought: but the Spirit itself maketh intercession for us with groanings which cannot be uttered.

27 And he that searcheth the hearts knoweth what is the mind of the Spirit, because he maketh intercession for the saints according to the will of God.

28 And we know that all things work together for good to them that love God, to them who are the called according to his purpose.

29 For whom he did foreknow, he also did predestinate to be conformed to the image of his Son, that he might be the firstborn among many brethren.

30 Moreover whom he did predestinate, them he also called:

and whom he called, them he also justified: and whom he justified, them he also glorified.

31 What shall we then say to these things? If God be for us, who can be against us?

32 He that spared not his own Son, but delivered him up for us all, how shall he not with him also freely give us all things?

33 Who shall lay any thing to the charge of God's elect? It is God that justifieth.

34 Who is he that condemneth? It is Christ that died, yea rather, that is risen again, who is even at the right hand of God, who also maketh intercession for us.

35 Who shall separate us from the love of Christ? shall tribulation, or distress, or persecution, or famine, or nakedness, or peril, or sword?

36 As it is written, For thy sake we are killed all the day long; we are accounted as sheep for the slaughter.

37 Nay, in all these things we are more than conquerors through him that loved us.

38 For I am persuaded, that neither death, nor life, nor angels, nor principalities, nor powers, nor things present, nor things to come,

39 Nor height, nor depth, nor any other creature, shall be able to separate us from the love of God, which is in Christ Jesus our Lord.

This chapter is just one of the chapters we can go to for instructions on walking in the spirit. We must keep our spirit nourished with the right spiritual food in order to grow, amen? Although we are in the world, we are not OF the word, so in order to walk in the newness of life, we must guard our spirit by walking in the spirit so that way, we will not fulfill the lust of the flesh. Amen, when people go out there and make a mess of themselves, whether it be sex out of wedlock and getting pregnant or getting someone else pregnant, or contracting a disease, when someone go out there and have a drink of alcohol until they pass out, when someone go and gamble their bill money away, ect....somebody has to clean the mess up!!!!!

Are we equipped to clean our own messes up? NO! We do not have the power to clean up our mess. Jesus is the only one who can wipe up our messes, not leaving a stain, like that red juice spilled in the carpet that we wiped up but the spot is still faintly seen. Jesus will wipe our mess completely up, not just COVER IT, but wipe it up never to be seen again! That's good isn't it?
 How you may ask?
Some things come by fasting and praying
Also Deliverance:
Matt 8:28-34
28 And when he was come to the other side into the country of the Gergesenes, there met him two possessed with devils, coming out of the tombs, exceeding fierce, so that no man might pass by that way.
29 And, behold, they cried out, saying, What have we to do with thee, Jesus, thou Son of God? art thou come hither to torment us before the time?
30 And there was a good way off from them an herd of many swine feeding.
31 So the devils besought him, saying, If thou cast us out, suffer us to go away into the herd of swine.
32 And he said unto them, Go. And when they were come out, they went into the herd of swine: and, behold, the whole herd of swine ran violently down a steep place into the sea, and perished in the waters.
33 And they that kept them fled, and went their ways into the city, and told every thing, and what was befallen to the possessed of the devils.
34 And, behold, the whole city came out to meet Jesus: and when they saw him, they besought him that he would depart out of their coasts.
(KJV)
This is just to give you an idea of how the mess that we can make with ourselves have to be cleaned...and just as I said in my entry from Friday, even just looking at something off limits to us can cause chaos and cause us to make a mess that Jesus has to clean up. Be careful of your messes; be careful of where

you take your spirit and the things that you put in your spirit. Pollutants harm!!!!!
Think about the environment and what pollutants does.....
Think about how sick we could get if we eat contaminated substances....
Think about if we do not drink enough water, (we can get dehydrated),
Think about if we eat all kinds of food and do not exercise..... (we can get overweight),
Amen now think about if we make a mess of our spiritual beings.....
it is no different than the way we can harm our physical bodies. Glory to God. Jesus is the mess cleaner; he'll pick us up, wash us, renew us, and put his spirit inside of us. But, we got to keep that spirit fed and nourished with the right things or else, we can pollute it, grieve it and quench it. Glory? Watch your walk, watch your talk, watch your going out and coming ins....many people do not think this is an important aspect to our spiritual growth.
Many think they can still watch any and everything that comes on TV.
listen to any and every kind of music....
not pray as much....
not fast......just to name a few
Amen. The Co-Founder of this ministry and I was talking about this same topic on yesterday. What happens to a car if you don't fill it up with gas? What happens to gasoline on the ground that you throw matches on? What happens to furniture if you do not take care of it? What happens to cornbread in the oven if you leave it on too long?
Amen, think about your spirit and what will happen if you stop depending on Jesus and leaning on your own strength, thinking everything is okay and listening to the devil telling you...
It's alright to listen to this secular music and look at a movie with cursing, ect....what harm can it do?
It's alright to indulge in this activity, what harm can it do? It's not the actual act, so you can get by with this, go head! It won't

hurt!
It's alright to go to sleep and not read a little of your word, God understands that you get tired!
JUST TO NAME A FEW.....
Do not be deceived by the tactics of the enemy!
Galatians 6:7 Be not deceived; God is not mocked: for whatsoever a man soweth, that shall he also reap.
8For he that soweth to his flesh shall of the flesh reap corruption; but he that soweth to the Spirit shall of the Spirit reap life everlasting.
9And let us not be weary in well doing: for in due season we shall reap, if we faint not.
10As we have therefore opportunity, let us do good unto all men, especially unto them who are of the household of faith.
11Ye see how large a letter I have written unto you with mine own hand.
12As many as desire to make a fair shew in the flesh, they constrain you to be circumcised; only lest they should suffer persecution for the cross of Christ.
13For neither they themselves who are circumcised keep the law; but desire to have you circumcised, that they may glory in your flesh.
14But God forbid that I should glory, save in the cross of our Lord Jesus Christ, by whom the world is crucified unto me, and I unto the world.
15For in Christ Jesus neither circumcision availeth any thing, nor uncircumcision, but a new creature.
16And as many as walk according to this rule, peace be on them, and mercy, and upon the Israel of God.
17From henceforth let no man trouble me: for I bear in my body the marks of the Lord Jesus.
18Brethren, the grace of our Lord Jesus Christ be with your spirit. Amen.
Praise the Lord, I am going to end this chapter right here, for I did not know where this was going, but the Holy Ghost does the leading and I do the following. I pray that this entry blesses somebody out there tonight as it has blessed me....on this

journey, we all must stand to be corrected when we get off the path of the straight and the narrow....it's not about us and never will it be....God instructs and correct his children and when we receive his correction, it's up to us to acknowledge our weak areas, confess and turn away from those things. Glory?
May God have a blessing upon the reader but most of all the doer of his holy word.

Chapter Eight
The Heart Is Deceitful and Desperately Wicked, Who Can Know It?
(ALL CAPS USED TO ADD EMPHASIS)

In the previous chapters, I posted some of my blog content. I pray that you have been blessed by each and every word written on those pages. Jeremiah17: 9 The heart is deceitful above all things, and desperately wicked: who can know it?
10 I the LORD search the heart, I try the reins, even to give every man according to his ways, and according to the fruit of his doings.
Praise God, the conviction of the church is somewhat ABSENT in this last hour. The hour that we should be seeking God like never before, and not just patching and botching up, but asking God to COMPLETELY FIX those areas that are not pleasing to him, we are seeking for somebody to feed us word that's going to cause us to jump, shout, sing, clap, ect....but does nothing to convict our souls and cause us to fall on our faces and repent of our sins and deliver us from bondages of the devil. Yeah, that's what I call THOSE FEEL GOOD MESSAGES! Time out for feeling good, it's time to repent for the kingdom of heaven is at hand! It's time to allow Jesus to inspect the conditions of our heart and if it's not in good standing, we have to allow him to give us a heart transplant!
God work me up around 5:17 and I was not able to go back to

sleep. I lay back down in my bed and the Holy Spirit began ministering to me about "THE CONDITION OF THE CHURCH IN ITS BACKSLIDDEN CONDTION...." And the preachers that preach the message, "ONCE SAVED ALWAYS SAVED!" Let me tell you today Saints of God who hold that mentality, throw that doctrine out of the window, because THAT'S NOT TRUE! THAT'S A SPIRIT OF DECEPTION! DON'T BE DECEIVED WITH THAT MESSAGE! We see here in Jeremiah 17:9~The Heart is deceitful above all things and desperately wicked: Who Can Know It?

How many years have we been deceived by our religious traditions? How many times have we been fed messages without checking it out to see if it lines up with the word of God? How many times have we let others come to us saying "they have a word of God for us...." and prophesied to our flesh and not to our spirit causing us to examine the conditions of our heart and mind and fall on our faces to repent if we are not in good standing with God?" Where is the rod of correction in the body? What is the condition of our heart?

We're all work and no play, building ministries, establishing churches, putting on conferences, seminars, talking about kingdom building, but are WE REALLY DOING IT FOR BUILDING THE KINGDOM OF GOD AND FOR THE PURPOSE OF WINNING LOST SOULS TO CHRIST? OR ARE WE BUILDING THEM TO RECEIVE A NAME, TO SEE HOW MANY COME AND PARTICIPATE, AND TO RECEIVE THAT PAT ON THE BACK?

We put on a event what is supposed to be for the Lord or so we say, and then when things don't turn out right, we pout, we get upset because things didn't turn out the way that WE WANTED IT TO GO. Not even bothering to ask is God pleased with what we are doing.

YES, WE MINISTER TO OTHERS TO HAVE A PERSONAL REALTIONSHIP WITH THE LORD, BUT WHAT ABOUT US AS MINISTERS HAVING A PERSONAL RELATIONSHIP WITH HIM ALONE WITHOUT THE GLITTER GLAMOUR OF OUR NAMES AND MINISTRIES?
WE'RE NOT GOING TO GET JUDGED BY OUR WORKS! GOOD WORKS WILL NOT GET US INTO THE KINGDOM OF HEAVEN. DON'T BE DECEIVED!

Matthew 7: 21 Not everyone who says to Me, "Lord, Lord," shall enter the kingdom of heaven, but he who does the will of My

Father in heaven.
22 Many will say to Me in that day, "Lord, Lord, have we not prophesied in Your name, cast out demons in Your name, and done many wonders in Your name?"
23 And then I will declare to them, "I never knew you; depart from Me, you who practice lawlessness."
We're living in a society now, especially in the ministry where some of leaders want to get that pat on the back and get that recognition to promote them and their ministry~all about building foundations and dynasties for ourselves. Everything revolves around us, but what about the SOULS?
We can build seventy five ministries and build churches in every country on this planet, but if our foundations is not built in and on Christ, then they are just ministries and churches, VOID OF GOD!
We can build churches and ministries in the name of Jesus, cast out demons in the name of Jesus, prophecy in the name of Jesus, and do many wonders in the name of Jesus, but just because WE USE HIS NAME DOES NOT MEAN HE'S IN WHAT WE ARE DOING! That will be a very disheartening thing to get told after doing all of that depart from me, you who practice lawlessness! Make dead sure your foundation is built on Christ and that you have a personal relationship with him!
Jesus told his disciples: Rejoice, not, that the spirits are subject unto you, but rather rejoice, because your names are written in heaven. Luke 10:20 ~Emphasis added
He was telling them not to rejoice at what they can do in his name, but to rejoice because their names was written in heaven! He's not pleased by the spirits being subject to us, that's fine and dandy, but HE **WANTS US TO BE IMPRESSED BY OUR NAMES BEING WRITTEN IN HEAVEN!** A person that controls the reins of his heart and controls his thought patterns pleases God!
Remember: The heart is deceitful above all things and desperately wicked, who can know it?
The church tries to constantly paint a picture to the world that all is perfect with us, we come decked out in our Sunday's best, hair do's and fresh hair cuts, makeup intact, hearing message

after message preached, singing Zion songs until heaven get the news, speaking in tongues, dancing around the church, but are WE SURE GOD'S THERE AND IN WHAT WE ARE DOING?
We preach at each other and test one another to see what kind of word we got, so we could instantly COMPARE OURSELVES TO EACH OTHER. It's all about US TRYING TO PROVE A POINT TO ONE ANOTHER INSTEAD OF TO GOD!
I HAD TO ASK MYSELF~All of the singing that I do, ministering to others, teaching of God's word, ect....have I really stopped and asked God was

MY HEART IN GOOD STANDING WITH HIM?

Am I really and truly delivered? After reading the contents of this book, have you asked that of yourself too?
I AM STILL HUMAN JUST LIKE YOU, AND I HAVE TO WORK OUT MY OWN SOUL'S SALVATION JUST LIKE YOU.

God have allowed me to see something's about my own walk, and about all of the glitter glamour of the ministry that is coming forth, and he has allowed me to evaluate it to see if it's for HIS GLORY or for MY GLORY. SEE I CAN TELL MY STORY BECAUSE I WANT TO BE RIGHT, NOT JUST PARTIALLY BUT TOTALLY. How many times have I given someone a word at their demand instead of at the demands of God? Oh Jesus, how many times have I prayed for others at their demand instead of God's will for that person's life.....see we got the mentality of being servants and being saved and meaning well, but

WE HADN'T FULLY GRASPED THE CONCEPT, THAT WE ARE NOT HERE TO BUILD OUR OWN THING AND TO VENTURE OFF AND DO WHAT WE WANT TO DO AND WHAT OTHERS WANT **US TO DO PER THEIR REQUEST**, BUT WE ARE HERE TO AID IN THE VISION OF OUR HEAVENLY FATHER, AND TO FINISH THE WORK THAT JESUS STARTED WHEN HE WALKED THE EARTH.....ALL FOR GOD'S GLORY AND OBEYING THE FATHER AND NOT MAN!
WHILE WE'RE ACCOMPLISHING THAT GOAL OF FINISHING THAT VISION, WE MUST HAVE A PERSONAL RELATIONSHIP WITH JESUS FOR OURSELVES!!!! EVERYTHING FOR GOD'S GLORY AND NOT FOR OUR OWNSELVES!
DON'T LET YOUR HEART DECIEVE YOU INTO THINKING THAT WORKS IS GOING TO GET YOU A CROWN IN HEAVEN! WE HAVE TO HAVE A PERSONAL REALTIONSHIP

WITH HIM! WE GOT TO KNOW HIM, NOT KNOW OF HIM, WE GOT TO LIVE FOR HIM, AND NOT JUST LIVE PARTIALLY IN HIM. ~SEE WHAT HAPPEND TO THE DEVIL WHEN HE WAS IN HEAVEN, HE TRIED TO EXALT HIMSELF ABOVE GOD~THOUGHT HE HAD EVERYTHING ALL SEWED UP TOGETHER BY THINKING NOTHING WAS GOING TO HAPPEN TO HIM, YOU SEE THERE WAS NO MORE PLACE FOUND FOR HIM IN HEAVEN, AND HE GOT KICKED OUT!
WE CAN'T THINK THAT WE ARE GETTING BY; RECEIVING THE CREDIT FOR GOD'S WORK, AND BUILDING KINGDOMS FOR JESUS THAT HE IS NOT IN! WE HAVE A JOB TO DO SAINTS OF GOD, NOT FOR OURSELVES, BUT FOR THE WORLD THAT IS DYING LOST~WHEN WE DRAW THOSE LOST SOULS, WE HAVE TO HAVE A PLACE TO DRAW THEM TO. WE CAN'T DRAW THEM TO A PLACE WHERE JESUS IS NOT EVEN PRESENT! WE MUST DRAW THEM TO A PLACE WHERE JESUS IS THERE SO HE CAN DO A WORK IN THEM!
CHURCH LET'S GET IT RIGHT SO WE CAN GO HOME, LET'S GO BACK TO OUR FIRST LOVE, LET'S STAND ON OUR FOUNDATION WHICH IS THE WORD OF GOD, AND LET'S NOT ONLY PREACH, TEACH, SING, SHOUT, SPEAK IN TOUNGUES, AT SERMON TIME OR ON SUNDAY, BUT LET US HAVE A PERSONAL ONE ON ONE FELLOWSHIP WITH THE LORD PERSONALLY!
THE HEART IS DECEITFUL ABOVE ALL THINGS AND IS DESPERATELY WICKED: WHO CAN KNOW IT?
WHAT IS THE CONDITION OF YOUR HEART? WHERE IS IT? WHAT ABOUT YOUR MIND? DO YOU OPERATE OUT OF THE REALM OF YOUR HEART OR YOUR MIND?

    We are born with the old sinful heart intact. {Born into sin}. Our hearts are deceptive, and in coming to Christ, we must ask God to replace the old carnal heart with the new heart. I'm not talking about a physical heart, but a spiritual heart. We see the plea of David's cry in Psalm 51:1 Have mercy upon me, O God, according to thy loving-kindness: according unto the multitude of thy tender mercies blot out my transgressions. He recognized God's generous love and his unending grace and mercy and he wanted God to wipe out his bad record. Psalm 51:2 goes on to say: Wash me thoroughly from mine iniquity, and cleanse me from my sin. Do you see the earnest request of David's plea to God? It's as though you can feel the intensity and sincerity of his words jumping off the page at you. Okay, now let's go a bit farther into verse 3. Notice that David acknowledge his transgressions and sins: Psalm 51:3 For I acknowledge my transgressions: and my sin is ever before me. It's as though he was saying, scrub away my guilt, and soak my sins in your laundry. I'm naked before you spiritually dear Lord, for my sins are every before me. We see here that David was truly sorrowful for his sins. That's how we must be in our confession of our sins! God knows if we are sincere or not. We must ACKNOWLEDGE our sins, and confess where we have gone wrong just as David did. Let's go a little farther, for I do not want you to miss anything in this reader. Verse 4 goes on to say; Against thee, thee only, have I sinned, and done this evil in thy sight: that thou mightest be justified when thou speakest, and be clear when thou judgest. Notice here, he didn't put the blame off on someone else, but he told God that it was against HIM ONLY did he sin. (He's took full responsibility for his iniquity,) he also acknowledged that God did indeed see it all, even if he wouldn't have confessed it, God still knew what he had done! God is all knowing reader. There's nothing on this earth that we do that he doesn't see! God wants to see if we will take full responsibility for our actions and not put the blame off on someone else. Okay let's move farther and see what he asked God to do for him. Psalm 51:5 Behold, I was shapen in iniquity; and in sin did my mother conceive me. "I was shapen in iniquity…" What is David saying here? He is saying since he was born, he has been in the wrong. We don't come into this world programmed to do that which is right. We are born with the sinful and deceitful natures of our hearts; we need new hearts and renewed minds! Let's go forward. Psalm 51:6 says; Behold, thou desirest truth in the inward parts: and in the hidden part thou shalt make me to know wisdom.7Purge me with hyssop, and I shall be clean: wash me, and I shall be whiter than snow. 8Make me to hear joy and gladness; that the bones which thou hast broken may rejoice.9Hide thy face from my sins, and blot out all mine iniquities. 10Create in me a clean heart, O God; and renew a right spirit within me. He was asking God to enter him and conceive a new true life. We need to ask God to enter us and conceive new true lives! The church has been walking around with the old hearts still intake, trying to see spiritual things with the old carnal heart and un-renewed minds. In order to understand what the spirit is saying to us in this hour, we need a new heart! God made man upright, his mind was clear and filled with that of heavenly things and not carnal things. He had a natural heart after God's own heart. Deceitfulness was not found in his heart. When he last the favor of God in the Garden of Eden, sin was birth forward. We hide behind the makeup, the dresses, the suits, the haircuts, the fancy hair-do's, the nail acrylic, ect...but what we are hiding is the true nature of our hearts. If every man and woman in the church was to reveal the true intents of their heart, we would turn the house of the Lord into a trashcan instead of God's house. Every little desire, lust, evil intent, self-conceit, vanity, pride, dishonest and unclean thing will be revealed. Oh, but it's a day that's coming, [Judgment Day] where every man's heart and deep dark secrets will be revealed. Our hearts will be revealed for what it really is. So if you are not delivered from bondage, guess what? It's going to be exposed! I can only tell the story of being in sexual bondages for that is what I went through. I just want to paint a picture to you reader that every struggle in the flesh that is not of God is a bondage that must be rid of!

Chapter 10
Soul-Ties

Good soul-ties are formed when two are more persons become bonded together. For instance: members of a church, a family, ect...Good soul-ties are founded upon the foundation of love which the Bible calls "the law of Christ" Gal. 6:2, and "the royal law" Jas. 2:8. The soul ties approved by God represent the bonding of persons together in agape love. In marriage, God purposes that a man and a woman be joined together to become one flesh. Ephesians 5:31~they are to be joined by love. God ordained sexual intercourse for marriage only! Marriage sexual union is an _expression approved by God. We see in Matthew 19:6 that divorce destroys those soul-ties that God created. The tearing causes, pain, trauma, and hurt and sorrow in the divorce.

Demonic soul-ties are the perversion of good and the holy. Demonic soul-ties are founded upon lust whereas, good soul-ties are founded upon love. When Satan sees an opportunity, he will pervert that which is pure. Fornication Ties- Do you not know that he who is joined to a harlot is one body with her? For 'The two', He says, 'shall become one flesh'" I Cor. 6:16. Through sexual relationships outside of marriage, demonic soul-ties are formed. Many people that have committed fornication may find themselves longing for past lovers, or thinking of the acts committed with those persons because they are TIED! Their souls are fragmented to those persons. So for instance: If you have committed fornication with three men or three women in your past, then you have left part of your soul with them. This create a bondage of un-healthy soul-ties. Let me explain farther: those who engage in sexual intercourse outside of marriage become the one flesh that God ordained in marriage. Whether you want to accept this or not, that's up to you, that's fine, but if you do not divorce your husbands or your wives that you have committed fornication with, you will not get out of bondage until you free yourself from your fornicating partners! If you don't know what fornication is; it's sex out of wedlock! Ungodly Soul-ties are also formed through that of same sex couples. The word of God declares their motivation behind this as lust and not love! Even their women changed the natural use for what is against nature: Likewise also the men, leaving the natural use of the woman, burned in their lust for one another" Rom. 1:26,27 (emphasis added).

Ties with Evil Companions: 1 Corinthians 15:33 reads; Be not deceived: evil communications corrupt good manners. It is very important to choose righteous and holy friends. Un-healthy Soul-ties with evil friends will put you in s snare and you will find yourself caught up in wickedness. Proverbs 22:5 reads; Thorns and snares are in the way of the froward: he that doth keep his soul shall be far from them.

Perverted Family Ties- The Bible declares that a man leave his father and mother and be joined with his wife. When a father gives his daughter away in marriage, he severs the soul-tie with her. If the tie is not broken, possessiveness and control are rendered and may become evil. On the other hand, one must never stop honoring his or her father and mother which is one of the ten commandments. Exodus 20:12 reads; Honour thy father and thy mother: that thy days may be long upon the land which the LORD thy God giveth thee.

Reader, I pray that you see your need for deliverance from un-healthy soul-ties. I pray that you are blessed by the words on these pages from my personal blog and straight from the Lord to you. I am going to close out with more of my blog entries as well as a deliverance prayer for you to pray. Please spread the word to those in your church homes and in your ministries, the importance of confessing the roots of bondages and asking God to sever those un-healthy soul ties.

God's Love

Behold, what manner of love the Father hath bestowed upon us, that we should be called the sons of God: therefore the world knoweth us not, because it knew him not. Beloved, now are we the sons of God, and it doth not yet appear what we shall be: but we know that, when he shall appear, we shall be like him; for we shall see him as he is. 1 John 3:1-2

What greater love can you find that's greater than that? We are people that's hungry for love and we want to experience this special kind of love, one that satisfies our hunger, thirst, and need to feel complete. But what we must understand that this kind of love is only given from God above. What we must realize is that we can't seek this kind of love from earthly men or women, but only from God above. The Father rained, poured, engulfed and showered his love upon us, so that we should be called the sons of God. That's some divine love isn't it? Are you glad to be a child of God? I'm not talking about just knowing OF him, but having a personal relationship with him. Anyone can know his name and know what he's capable of doing, but until we have a personal relationship with him, then we can proudly say that WE KNOW HIM BECAUSE

WE HAVE A PERSONAL REALTIONSHIP WITH HIM. Glory to God. The world do not know this kind of love because they do not know God. That's why you see many desperately seeking for this love that only God can give because they do not know God, for if they REALLY KNEW HIM, they will be desperately seeking for the love that only he can give, doing what's required to please HIM, satisfying HIM, living and breathing HIM, if we would spend so much of our energy that we do searching for this bestowed love in earthly people, then we would really began to see the manfiestations of God working in our lives and not looking for love anywhere else but in him.

We have not because we ASK NOT. We must understand that we must seek first the kingdom of God and all of HIS righteousness, then will he add things unto us, but all and all, this special kind of love that I'm referring to cannot be sought out in the world. All throughtout the New Testament, you see scriptures declaring "God's Love." Even 1 Corinthians 13 list a whole chapter about love. So you must understand that having the love of God in us is something that's not just a requirement but it should be instilled in us allowing us to freely give it as becoming born again Christians filled with the HolyGhost, for without it everything else is vain and useless. If we do not have the love of God, then how can we really love others? If we do not have the Holy Ghost how can we know this love?

Here are some scriptures that fathom God's love and requires us to have this same love.

1 John 4:10 Herein is love, not that we loved God, but that he loved us, and sent his Son to be the propitation for our sins.

Ephesians 5:2 And walk in love, as Christ also hath loved us, and hath given himself for us an offering and a sacrifice to God for a sweetsmelling savour.

Galatians 1:3-4 Grace be to you and peace from God the Father, and from our Lord Jesus Christ. Who gave himself for our sins, that he might deliver us from this present evil world, according to the will of God and our Father.

Romans 8:35 Who shall separate us from the love of Christ? shall tribulation, or distress, or persecution or famine, or nakedness, or

peril, or sword?
Romans 5:8 But God commendeth his love toward us, in that, while we were yet sinners, Christ died for us.
That's the foundation of our relationship with God. It's built on that love that God commendeth. He didn't commend it FOR us, but TO us. Anyone can say they love you, but without showing that love or commending that love to someone, then that love is vain, empty, and useless.
Actions speak louder than word. We see throughout the Bible, that God has backed his commendeth love toward us. He's loving, merciful, kind, gracious, good, wonderful, extravagant, I'll be here all day just explaining what God is to me and even for ones that don't recognize what he is and who he is. This thing is personal, for you must realize for yourself what God is to you, for I know what he is to me.
He just didn't say that he loved us and didn't prove that love to us. Glory to God. God's love is more than what we can ever imagine that it is, it can't be understood in the natural, it can't be understood in the flesh. That's why the world don't know us because they don't know him. Yeah, they may know OF him, but they don't know him for if they really did, then they would turn away from sin and surrender completely to him. That's why the world seek for love in the flesh, not realizing that the flesh is not made for this kind of love to be fathomed, the flesh is not made to be satisfied. Our spirits are made to understand this love, grasp this love, and be satisfied with this love. That's why you see so many women and men killing themselves behind spouses when the relationship doesn't work out, simply because they are trying to understand LOVE IN THE FLESH AND FIND THIS LOVE IN A EARTHLY MAN OR WOMAN. How about coming into the spirit so you can understand God's love? We need to tell the world about this kind of love, we must tell the world that God loves us and he doesn't require nothing in return but our hearts, souls and minds, and our "yes, Lord, I will do whatever I can to please you."
See the world loves you one day and the next minute or second, they may be tearing you down behind your back.

God doesn't say he loves you one minute and then the next minute, he tears you down and then build you back up again. Seek God's love, don't get comfortable with this earthly love, for earthly love can be sweet one day and bitter sweet the next, who wants bitter love? Who wants love that will wax cold?
I challenge you today Saints to understand God's love toward you. In order to understand his love, the flesh must be crucified, for the flesh is nowhere in this love. You have to walk in the spirit to understand this love. Romans 8:5 reads For they that are after the flesh do mind the things of the flesh; but they that are after the Spirit the things of the Spirit. 6 goes on to say, For to be carnally minded is death; but to be spiritually minded is life and peace. Glory to God, that's where the love is, the joy, the peace, the longsuffering, the meekness, the temperance, the faith, the gentleness and the goodness. It's found in the spirit and not in the flesh. You can't understand God's love unless you are spiritually minded.
What kind of mind are you harboring today? Do you understand God's love to you? Do you understand that the love that you are seeking is only found in Christ? I challenge you today Saints, to engulf yourself in the love of God and I promise you will never seek to find love anywhere else. May God have a blessing upon the reader, but most of all the doer of His Holy Word.
Prayer for Deliverance
Dear God, in the name of JESUS:
According to Romans 10:9 I confess with my lips that JESUS is Lord and in my heart I believe that You raised him from the dead. According to Luke 13:3; I repent of my past sins and I admit and confess that I have sinned (name) and I believe that You are faithful and just to cleanse me from all unrighteousness. I call upon You, Lord JESUS to cleanse me from all sin and unrighteousness by Your Blood (1 John 1:7). And as Your word says in Romans 10:13 Everyone who calls upon the name of the Lord will be saved.
I confess, repent and ask forgiveness of occult practices such as (witchcraft, fortune telling, horoscopes, astrology, water witching, etc.)
I renounce all occult practices and Satan and break all curses

associated with those occult practices. According to Galatians 3:13 Christ purchased our freedom [redeeming us] from the curse [doom] of the Law [and its condemnation] by [Himself] becoming a curse for us, for it is written [in the Scriptures], Cursed is everyone who hangs on a tree (is crucified); Deut. 21:23.
I confess, repent, and ask forgiveness of all sins listed in Deuteronomy 27 and 28 and break the curses associated with these sins.
I confess, repent and ask forgiveness of my iniquities and my fathers' iniquities according to Leviticus 26:40 and I break the curses associated with these iniquities.
I break and loose myself from all evil soul ties with my mother, father, brother, sisters, spouses, former spouses, former sex partners, etc.
Lord JESUS: I forgive my mother, father, brothers (name), sisters (name) and _____ and anyone else who has ever hurt me. Matthew 6:15, 18:21, 22, 35; Luke 11:4 (Lord's prayer).
I break and loose myself and my family from all curses that have been and are being placed upon me and my family: curses of witchcraft, physic thoughts or prayers, ungodly intercessory prayers, and words spoken in anger and I return these curses to the sender(s) sevenfold and bind them upon them by the blood of JESUS. In JESUS Name, Amen.[1]

All in the name of Jesus I come to you,
~Evangelist Shanetria
A Vessel Coming With Purpose

Note

Many of you in the body of Christ may be struggling with masturbation a sin that many are unsure of whether it's what's right or wrong. I want you to use your sense of judgment here. God created sex for marriage right? So in masturbation, the same exact pleasure that is felt in sex is experienced by one person without a partner. As Christians, we need to be growing toward perfection even in our thoughts. For if you live according to the flesh (by giving in to its desires), you will die" and tells us how to stop, "but if by the Spirit you put to death the misdeeds of the body, you will live" (Romans 8:13). In Masturbation, you are still able to achieve the results, (climax or orgasm) as you would with a sexual partner. Masturbation is a way of loving self and pleasing only self, when sex was clearly created to be enjoyed with a husband or wife.

"Just as you used to offer the parts of your body in slavery to impurity and to ever-increasing wickedness, so now offer them in slavery to righteousness leading to holiness. When you were slaves to sin, you were free from the control of righteousness" (Romans 6:19-20). When we offer the parts of our body to sin, we become slaves to sin. Romans 6:13 reads; Neither yield ye your members as instruments of unrighteousness unto sin: but yield yourselves unto God, as those that are alive from the dead, and your members as instruments of righteousness unto God. "Those who live according to the flesh have their minds set on what the flesh desires; but those who live in accordance with the Spirit have their minds set on what the Spirit desires" (Romans 8:5). God created sex and he created us with sex drives, but he created the union of sex for marriage only! This was his gift to married couples and not for us to use for personal gratification. In the mind, the image of nudity is put into view whether it's of another person or of yourself, and as that view come more into view, the desire becomes more intense. That is a tool for the devil to use to set up a stronghold and a bondage that needs to be broken! If you are thinking of yourself and another person while committing this act, then you are literally having sex in your mind with the person that is not your husband or wife, and therefore: that creates a un-healthy soul tie that needs to be broken for you have became literally joined with that person in your heart. Jesus told us in Matthew 5:27 that; Whosoever looketh on a woman to lust after her hath committed adultery with her already in his heart. That's very powerful isn't it? We are to walk in the spirit, so that we will not fulfill the desires of the flesh. "So I say, live by the Spirit, and you will not gratify the desires of the flesh. For the sinful nature desires what is contrary to the Spirit, and the Spirit what is contrary to the sinful nature. They are in conflict with each other, so that you do not do what you want"(Galatians 5:16-17). Masturbation is clearly a sin because it doesn't come from faith. Christ is our ultimate example of how we are to live. His flesh was crucified, (he lived a sinless life), and not just controlled or suppressed! Sex is a desire and not a need. We cannot make it without food and water for it's a necessity, but we can live without sex! Sex is a desire giving only to married couples. Just because the word masturbation is not listed in the scriptures does not mean that it isn't wrong! We need to stop going around condoning sin, talking about, "Well, the Bible doesn't mention it so it's okay!" That's a sin to even measure your knowledge against that of God's! It is self explanatory, sex was created for a man and a woman and no other union! Not with a person not your husband and wife and not with yourself! Masturbation just as Porn is a doorway to bondage, and if you do not see this reader, you will not see your need for deliverance. Answer this question: If masturbation was so right, why do feelings of guilt set in afterwards? Do you think God wants us to walk around in shame and guilt? No he doesn't! His desire is for us to be free and not trapped in bondage. May God have a blessing upon the readers but most of all the doers of his holy word.

Yours in Christ

~Evangelist Shanetria

Evangelist Shanetria is the author of over several books and resides in the Southern US with her family.

www.ingramcontent.com/pod-product-compliance
Lightning Source LLC
Chambersburg PA
CBHW031357160426
42813CB00081B/100